OPPONG AMOABENG

FOREWORD BY DR. JOE IBOJIE

THE POSITIVE POWER *of* VISION

Keys for Cultivating Kingdom Attitudes to Operate and Achieve Your Dreams and Visions

ISBN: 978-9988-8720-0-7
ISBN eBook: 978-87-971340-7-8

For Worldwide Distribution, Printed in Europe

1 2 3 4 5 6 / 22 21 20 19

DEDICATION

To the millions of my friends and readers in the world,
whose strong desire is to find the reasons why they live,
I dedicate this book.

ENDORSEMENTS

The power of seeing and using the active sense of imagination is a result of an elevated revelatory sense, an intuitive sense born from a perceived spirit of the mind and heart, a unique sense in its disposition and output; hence, nothing precedes vision, purpose, and leadership. The Lord orders the steps of a good man. God orders our good steps because a good man submitted to Him. They submitted under His banner of grace and thus caught His frequency and movement. Men who caught sight of God caught sight of His will, vision, and purposes to be spiritually or divinely law-abiding, purposeful unto God and humanity.

A man who sees what God sees and imagines what God imagines will obtain accreditation from Heaven. Heaven will always assist such a person on assignment. This is how I would want to describe Rev. Oppong Amoabeng. He sees, he thinks, and he writes comprehensively. Particularly on the subject of vision, this book is a pearl. Reverend Oppong Amoabeng is such a phenomenal gift that has captured the core image of what he is teaching in this book— *The Power of Positive Vision*. I recommend this book to be read in all schools and theological platforms.

Rev. Acheampong Yiadom-Boakye
Senior Pastor, International Central Gospel Church (ICGC)
Strong Tower-Taifa, Accra, Ghana
Area Supervising Minister

Where there is no vision, the people perish. Vision is inevitably important to any group of people. It is therefore required that every leader and individual has a vision for his or her people and for him or herself, respectively. Nothing comes into reality without first being visualized. Writing a book about vision in the times we live in is timely. This book takes us through the vision process and motivates us to have a vision for our lives, the things we do, and especially what defines our passion. Rev. Oppong Amoabeng has laid it out so clearly and easy to understand. A must-read book for any serious person who wants to be positively relevant. I highly recommend *The Positive Power of Vision*.

Rev. Dr. James O. Commey
Senior Pastor
International Harvest Christian Center

The only thing worse than being blind is having sight but no vision.
—Helen Keller

This is an interesting quote from a blind person about the difference between having sight and having vision. Sight is a function of the eyes and allows us to see. This is something a blind person doesn't have, but the rest of us have. While she thinks it's bad, it could be worse. Vision, on the other hand, is in the mind or the mind's eye. It is a proactive portion of our imagination and helps us plan and think about our ideas. The quote states that while she is not happy with being unable to see, she feels it is better than being able to see, but not being able to imagine, to plan, to think beyond our meager existence.

In this book, *The Positive Power of Vision*, Rev. Oppong Amoabeng has brought us an understanding of what vision and sight mean. He has given us the blueprint of how to conceive our God-given vision and how to stay with this vision till it is fulfilled. As you read this very informative book, get ready to be transformed.

Eric Xexemeku,
(Resident Pastor)
ICGC-Open Heavens Temple, East-Legon, Accra, Ghana

Thy word is a lamp unto my feet, and a light unto my path.
—Psalms 119:105 KJV

Today more than ever, there is a need for Christians to return to the purpose for which they were created. In a seemingly confusing world, the Word of God provides the right focus needed to excel in our daily walk. With the right focus then comes the grace to be exceptional and the ability to stand out in our world. This book, *The Positive Power of Vision*, offers practical strategies describing salient ways by which our God-ordained purpose can be well understood and manifested. I strongly recommend this book because the world needs this message. It's a timely publication, diligently gathered by the author to encourage Christians to let their light shine.

H. E. Mrs. Amerley Ollennu Awua-Asamao
Ghana Ambassador,
Denmark & Nordic Countries

You are the light of the world. A city that is set on a hill cannot be hidden. Nor do they light a lamp and put it under a basket, but on a lampstand, and it gives light to all who are in the house.
—Matthew 5:14-15

God loves the whole world and He provides for its inhabitants by divinely investing great treasures. These treasures can be called universal investments of God toward mankind. I personally believe that time, gifts, and opportunities (in life) are essential requirements men are blessed with. The author has penned down impeccable truth on the power of vision in this book entitled, *The Positive Power of Vision.*

Genuinely, men light a lamp because men are the light of the world. The author sees visionaries as lampstands who give light, illumination, inspiration, and power to others. What you see matters; hence, read this book with keen interest. You'll see things in the perspective of God.

H. E. Rev. Mrs. Jane Gasu Aheto
The Ghana Ambassador to Guinea Conakry

ACKNOWLEDGMENTS

Every achievement in this world is as a result of human contribution of many people who directly and indirectly invested their gifts, talents and knowledge. This book is no exception. I am mostly indebted to my family and local church that gave me the opportunity to share the truth of the power of positive vision before it ever became a book on the shelf or an e-book on the net. I share the good experience of having been raised by my mother as a single parent in hazardous environments, yet I came out who I am and what I have become and stand for.

There are few people I cannot but thank greatly. C. I. Ogu from London, a friend who gave me moral support and constructive ideas; and helped in reading the entire manuscript. Rev. Claude Mann of Character Developers, Ghana, whose role as my Consulting Editor has brought a lot of transformation to my writing. I also express gratitude to Nii Addokwei Moffatt of Graphic Communications Group Limited, Ghana.

Most of all, I am grateful to God Almighty whose light guides us in the path of righteousness for His namesake.

TABLE OF CONTENTS

INTRODUCTION

The positive power of vision is the ability to develop a skill of seeing things correctly the way they ought to be seen. It is a perspective a person considers in life because it fits the description of God's ultimate will and sovereignty. The Bible reveals that God sees and works from the position of love toward His creation, particularly His love for humanity. It is through this divine point that His purpose and intent manifest in us and through us. A life lived under God only becomes better because God becomes the foundation, beam, and support for that person's God-oriented vision and purpose.

The ability to gain knowledge and understanding of God's will, intent, and purpose is a positive vision. This vision has tremendous and incredible power. Thus, anything one does outside God's vision and purpose is questionable and can be described as a negative vision. Life without vision or a negative vision and purpose is a fatal accident, an abuse, total waste, and a tragic tragedy.

In this way, that person will destroy the harmony of the earth with wrong and bad tunes. It is obvious that God has endowed all people on earth with great power and positive skill to see things in unique ways, which should go a long way to support His purpose and plans on earth. And when we do things according to God's intents, we emerge as unique individuals known for something we alone can do.

The divine gift of God gives us a trait of distinction. Satisfactory to God's sovereign will, He promotes us to transcend into excellent paradigms of extraordinariness where our visions speak. As human beings, we should not go missing among a lot of people, but we must stand out and be outstanding. We should be seen as different persons because of what we do differently. Normally, our different contributions are regarded as just a small part, but they help build a larger picture of life on earth. Often, the small things we learn to do right lead us to the greater things we do appreciably. And through our significant contributions, we become rare pearls highly priced on the world market. In this direction, it is vital to know that our visions, gifts, and demands sell us better as we nurture and develop ourselves.

It is necessary to mention that anytime a person sees something clearly from the beginning to the end and vice versa, it can be referred to as one's vision. Such a gift also means that each person will become a leader in his skill assignment and contribute to making our world a better place. The entire human race has a leadership spirit over creation (Genesis 1:26-28); and we need to discover and develop them in our spirit of leadership in order to realize this gem. Therefore, through the power of vision, or imaginative visualization, we can discover all our inherent powers.

The way to achieve true leadership is in the strength to tap into the future with the laws that govern sight. Sight itself as a natural component—including foresight, insight, hindsight, and ultimately, imaginative creativity—is the apparatus; these are elements that come in to give a proper definition of vision. So the reality is that vision and leadership are synonymous and no one can separate them and succeed. As visionaries and leaders, we can see and get what we always visualize by daring passionately a little more than the norm.

These endowed gifts can best manifest in our visual images for all streams and endeavors, particularly that of purposeful quality leadership orientation. A person with a God-given vision and with a pure direction can lead and help others in many ways. This is because he can assist and lead them to their required destinies. In every assignment on earth, there is the spirit of leadership, which one must discover by the positive power of vision. And this book offers the reader the basic tools by which our leadership assignments can be realized through everyone's respective customized vision.

In this case, leadership of every kind, both spiritual and natural, can only be realized in its truest form if they are motivated by a God-given direction. Every one of us is born in his or her generation because our purposes are needed in our respective periods. Hence, I believe that any source of human development, which is initiated without the will of God, is dangerous for man. Such gifts and abilities of leadership and vision may last for a little while and create permanent disappointment at the end if they are not aligned to the will and intent of God's purposes. Remember, the end matters most in every human initiative. And any God-given gift, which operates without His will and intent, creates destructive abuses. We must know that any initiated paradigm of abuse destroys mankind.

The gifts of life, whether spiritual or natural, follow almost the same pattern of development. If any individual's gift is enviable (in the sight of others), it is because that person has quality time for its development. You will realize that such a person is disciplined with an enriched attitude, which did not come to him or her on a silver platter, but through perspiration (hard work). In fact, there are two components of gift development. There is the inspiration paradigm and the perspiration paradigm. The former is God-endowed, and the latter is human-endowed. When the two forces are known and combined, success is inevitable.

In this regard, every vision takes a long period of time and effort before they come to manifestation. "For the vision is yet for an appointed time, but at the end it shall speak, and not lie: though it tarry, wait for it; because it will surely come, it will not tarry" (Habakkuk 2:3 KJV). It is equally important to stress that anytime a vision is realized, it gives meaning to past losses. In this case, we should not lose hope, but wait patiently and continue to believe in the great God who has called us. His promises never fail; He will trigger our vision to be accomplished at the appointed time.

Personally, I advocate that no person should neglect his or her calling or vision for any personal reasons. My reason for saying this is because the purpose of life becomes nothing when we reject any of our gifts, ministry, and assigned activity. Our visions remain dormant in us and eventually remain untapped, which will eventually be buried at the cemetery to keep enriching the place. It is assumed that the cemetery is the richest place on earth. It is considered the richest spot on earth because much human potential is buried and entrapped perpetually, never to be released for the benefits of mankind.

In this book, I encourage my readers to keep their vision alive because they can realize their dreams whether young or old. Let's take notice that the vision human beings visualize, reflects as their attitudinal traits. God has called everyone to do something with his or her life and one of the abilities is our capacity to dream. When human beings dream, they develop strength and wisdom, which helps them to also understand the huge dynamics of hyper-elevated mysteries around them and influence circumstances in God's instructive manner. This dream gift is found in all of us irrespective of our sinful nature and human inadequacies.

Parents as leaders and visionaries should serve as role models to their children and the society at large and they can do this if they have well-placed visions themselves. To have a well-placed vision is important because it can help give the young ones a sense of direction, good will, and hope in the purposes that rule in them. If we neglect the power of vision and work with our own limited human wisdom, we will not only fail the children but also generations unborn.

The Positive Power of Vision is a means by which leadership principles of God's Word can be realized and made relevant to suit our present-day life's challenges. Through this book, my humble passion is to see people transformed into leaders with a positive sense of vision. We can take active responsibility for the reasons why we have become leaders of the earth. And it goes without doubt that a good leader will influence society with his customized sense of leadership principles and transform servants to be powerful leaders. I also believe that everybody can be a channel of blessing to the world because we are all blessed people. In this assessment, each one of us should realize what he is blessed with. Our kind of blessing will determine and influence what we are supposed to do and where we must go.

On the other hand, I believe that everyone can become what he desires through hard work in accordance with his God-given vision. My purpose is to help many people through this book to remove the devil's blindfold so that everyone can see and understand the truth and power sense of vision.

I believe that we can all bring our God-given visions to realization through hard work and faithfulness to God. This book discusses how God-given visions can become real in our lives when we cultivate the habit and ethics of operating from an elevated sense. This book is about you and not about anyone else.

It is the gateway to the chances you have, the beliefs you must cultivate, the need to psyche yourself, the sight you must see, and the choices you have available in your daily decisions, presented in knowledge packs. Your destiny is about to experience what God made it to mean. You have a positive action to take and it will revolutionize your life forever. This is because you belong to the elite minority groups that have cultivated the wealth of positive elevation, sense, and the power of positive vision and actions.

FOREWORD

I have often found it curious when the Bible says a person dies "full of years." That presupposes that some others could die "not full of years." Understanding how years or days could probably be lost in a person's life is one of the topics covered in this book. The Bible says of patriarch Abraham, "Then Abraham breathed his last and died in a good old age, an old man **and full of years**, and was gathered to his people" (Genesis 25:8). And of Job, the Bible also says, "So Job died, old **and full of days**" (Job 42:17).

Any day or year anyone lives outside the purpose of God for his life is a day or year lost from the fullness of his age. This is because the Kingdom of Heaven is a thematic expression of God's eternal purpose for our lives. God's eternal purpose for us must be discovered and pursued.

I have known Pastor Oppong Amoabeng for some years. He is a brilliant Bible scholar, a family man, a seasoned pastor, and a prolific writer. He pays superb attention to details and has a pleasant personal disposition. The reader will find all these qualities reflected on the pages of this book.

His book, *The Positive Power of Vision*, is a timely release of profound revelations from the very throne of God. This book will help to open the reader's eyes and serve as a compass to navigate the boisterousness of life on earth. Pastor Oppong Amoabeng has put together a book that will inspire and motivate the reader to greater heights in life.

Life is not without its challenges and so pursuing your vision can be fraught with daunting obstacles, some tending to derail. This book will not only motivate you but will also help to ensure that you keep your fervency serving the Lord.

My friend Pastor Oppong Amoabeng has reached out to God and pulled from Heaven what all those who are pregnant with dreams and divine promises need to read so they can find wisdom and insight to help them bring their visions into the realities of their lives.

This book teaches the reader that purpose and vision are crucial and that to neglect them tantamounts to a wasteful display of ignorance. This book will bless you!

Late Dr. Joe Ibojie
Best Selling Author and Prophetic Teacher
Senior Pastor, The Father's House Church Network
Aberdeen, Scotland, UK
www.the-fathers-house.org.uk

Chapter 1

WHAT IS YOUR VISION? WHAT DO YOU SEE?

Many years ago, in a lecture at school, in one rare moment, my literature tutor paused, detoured from his subject, and said to the entire student body, "You guys must pick up a vision and begin to think in clear terms what your lives are going to amount to in the future. This is because I have realized how many of you become so busy in the future that you eventually become ineffective people."

This was a digression from our core lesson. It was an out-of-curriculum insight, yet this gem of a statement challenged me more than the lesson itself. As young students, most of us scorned at him and even nicknamed him "Mr. Lectures." However, I have grown, matured, and by hindsight have realized that "Mr. Lectures" was absolutely right. Today, by the benefit of hindsight, the misconception I had about him has been hacked down. As a masonry working on a patched wall, he was hacking down debris on our minds with the correct mortar. My doubts and scorns have been replaced with reflective and retrospective love and a wish to meet him and present him with a laurel.

Thus, a right act, even in a wrong place and time could create a permanent revelation on purpose and point people to the perspectives required for accomplished success. Knowing that one can be "too busy and never effective" in life was a great key a mentor handed over to me to help unlock my future doors and opportunities.

In those days, as a growing teenage student, I questioned the authenticity of his postulation as a mere display of rhetoric and knowledge. To me, he was intellectually arrogant, I supposed. How on earth are people ineffective yet busy? My own cultivated myopic inhibitions were not potent to deliver me from my weak thought of faith. Men-owned safety and deliverance do not start in their situation. They begin in their developed mind. Deliverance always starts from your mind. Your mentality brings deliverance more than any external factor can.

Frequently, I soliloquized and thought to myself, and many questions led me on to think about the future. I triggered my sense of imagination and captured a world I wanted to live in one day. Therefore, I studied and also developed a desire to find out the main reason why I existed as a human being so that I could become busy, efficient, and effective in my endeavors. Importantly, every person must learn how to keep their own mode of expression; nevertheless, transformation and change come by the visions they cultivate in their minds and hearts via the provocative utterances of their heads. Headship gifts can project and promote your leadership ability. These heads are your parents, teachers, civic leaders, and spiritual leaders.

I needed to know the reasons for my creation among other people in the world. I wanted to be satisfied and become efficient and effective in the discharge of my purpose and not live people's proposals. I sought to discover my true identity, abilities, and my purpose in order to become efficient and effective, and not just busy and ineffective. The most dangerous thing that could ever happen against you is to live and never discover why. There're too many whys anyway. Nevertheless, the most important of all the whys is why you live. Your reason for being is important for your success on earth. "Mr. Lectures" provoked me to seek my inner self and this is the vehicle that has transported me to the destination I am presently in.

I vowed to myself never to be ineffective as so many others end up in this world; that is, never be a normal person with normal desires and among normal people in all normal accomplishments. I could not be in the number and standout. But I could stand out of the number and be different. Even now I can only speculate how long it takes to have a way to normalcy or to recede from the fear of failure if I don't march up pound for pound every day to overcome my own inadequacies and inhibitions.

For that much, probing questions emerged out of my quest and passion for living an efficient, effective life on purpose. My facilitator's statement preoccupied my mind. "Busy and never effective"? No! Not me! I will be busy and effective in the future, and how do I become effective? I asked myself many questions in those days and I still do. It helped and helps me to stay focused, efficient, and effective as an individual. We can look at some of these questions that help effectiveness and efficiency in life and it will help every person who wants to be helped.

Why am I here on earth?

What is my vision and dream?

What can I do best in life?

How can I identify and discover the crucial purposes of God for my life before I die?

If everything is really created for a purpose, then what purpose do I serve where I find myself now?

As a creature, I should fit somewhere in the mind of the Creator; and where exactly do I fit?

I have a reason for being human; how can I discover this gem of blessing?

Alongside these searches, I have noticed that we can go for lessons and receive motivational instructions and attend all the possible seminars, but God gives us prolific ideas worth all our self-orientations and programs. Mind you, you're never a grown up to the ones that birthed you into life. They will consider you their unparalleled protégé. They will absolutely disregard the inevitable gray hair on your head and the blossoming aging features on your body and still treat you as their child.

And no matter how many kids will ever call you Dad or Mum, to them, you are still their boy or girl. They'll forever see you like that. Period.

This is how God wants us to call Him—Father—as we remain eternal children of His throne. God personalizes specific instructions and hands them over to us to fulfill our life's purposes and assignments. And I have not deviated in this book to point my readers to this fact. God loves to see you think that He's seen you slipped into the corridors of life and put on yourself grown-up clothes of maturity and are still just playing a game before Him because you ever come for thoughts and ideas to run your daily life on earth.

The Bible is the thoughts and ideas of God for your life on earth. God speaks to us because He understands the child in us as a father does. He speaks to our blanket blatant-clutching, thumb-sucking infantile behaviors, and needs alike. In spite of your growth, fame, income, job description, education, and societal notoriety, God is always your Father in Heaven. As the Father, He looks deep into your innermost being and sees your hidden burdens and innermost needs. How funny when God sees your matured life as His child and you are still in need of candies and chocolates, which He's willing to supply. God sees and is aware of your lurking shadows of childish desires; for a father gives supplies and directions through the spectacle of your mind's eyes.

And before we proceed in acquiring knowledge on the positive power of vision, I wish we learn from Proverbs 29:18 (KJV). King Solomon wrote to his subjects in Israel and to the entire world saying, "Where there is no vision, the people perish: but he that keepeth the law, happy is he." According to the American Standard Version of the Bible this verse states, "Where there is no vision, the people cast off restraint; But he that keepeth the law, happy is he."

I urge that we memorize this piece of Scripture until it becomes a part of our thinking and imagination. We can be very effective, efficient, and purposeful people through the basic wisdom of gaining understanding and divine insight. Note that we must be effective people on earth; not just busy ones. The fact is that every person born in this world was created to undertake a specific task that no one else is born to accomplish.

And that particular task, when discovered and fulfilled, will make him or her an unforgettable individual on earth. There are some names that when mentioned bring to our minds some good deeds and those deeds may probably be the specific reasons behind the creation of those people. I have also quoted this particular Scripture severally in this book because the entire book entitled, *The Positive Power of Vision*, is based on the theme and I want my readers to tune in to the spirit of vision and get transformed from the ordinary rudiments of life in this world.

WHAT IS VISION

Vision, according to the current edition of A.S. Hornby's *Oxford Advanced Learner's Dictionary*, "is the power of seeing or imagining, looking ahead or grasping the truth that underlies facts."

The Oxford Desk Dictionary also defines vision as "the act or faculty of seeing...in a dream or trance, which is of supernatural or prophetic apparition. Thing or idea perceived vividly in the imagination; an imaginative insight."

The *Concise Oxford English Dictionary* explains vision as "the act or faculty of perceiving with the eye - the image one gets just as on television." But this time it occurs in one's mind; the ability or an instance of great perception.

In this way, your thought becomes more important than the mind as it carries thoughtful ideas and moves them into compartmentalized degrees of sights. The definition of vision connotes "seeing," yet it goes beyond that. And as the Bible is founded on the Hebrew and Greek languages with Aramaic interludes, it may probably be of worth to consult, excavate, and draw inspiration from these languages as a vital tool for knowledge and insightful revelation.

Therein, one discovers a gem of powerful and insightful understanding regarding the word vision. Vision is an encapsulation of powerful ingredients and elements, which goes beyond just seeing. Of course, vision protects us from being very busy and not highly effective people.

When we take time to understand the features and values of vision we evolve as effective tools in God's hands. That is, we "**come into being**."

The Old Testament Hebrew word *hazon* translated means "**to see**" and in reality, all focused images one develops become progressive and advance toward future times. The Greek word for vision is *opticia*, through which we developed the English words optical and optician, which revolve around the element of sight and seeing.

The Latin word for vision is *video,* by which the English word video is obtained. Thus, from these languages and biblical perspectives, vision means **the ability to see** and **synchronize one's thought and being** as an **integration of what one sees** to make the **beginning and end meaningful** as regard to what is seen toward future accomplishments for human elevation, advancement, and progress.

WHAT OTHERS SAY ABOUT VISION

As Rick Warren states in his book, *The Purpose Driven Church* (Grand Rapids, Zondervan, 1995, 29), "Most people think of 'vision' as the ability to see the future. But in today's rapidly changing world, vision is also the ability to accurately assess current changes and take advantage of them. Vision is the ability to see the opportunities within your current circumstance" and make good use of them.

Vision is an image formed that is pictured within the mind's eyes of an individual. The power of seeing and imagining what you desire and working it out (getting it) in the tied up future avenues and time, offers us bright possibilities. Vision is the driving force and the secret behind the success of nations and persons who call the shots in today's world! (Anonymous)

Myles Munroe defines vision as "foresight with insight based on hindsight," and he also believes that "when you discover your vision, it will give you energy and passion; vision is the ability to see things as they should be. The vision in your heart will spark that which will enable you to pursue your dream…vision sets goals, which motivates a plan of action" (see *The Principles and Power of Vision*, Whitaker House, 2003, 31-32, 41, and *In Pursuit of Purpose*, Destiny Image, 2015, 83).

MY PERSONAL DEFINITION OF VISION

I define vision as the systematic, step-by-step fulfillment of a person's God-given revelation, dreams, and imaginations through effective and efficient faith-oriented thinking systems, kingdom-aligned cultural beliefs, hard work, determination, and faithfulness in order to fulfill the course assignment and purpose of life. Every "thus saith the Lord" projects a vision for your increased pursuit and your diligence, hard work, prayer, and good conduct increased under the eyes of God, all of which will generate an appointed time for an "it came to pass."

A strong visionary builds his life on God's eternal purposes, not in self-thoughtfulness, skill, ability, education, gimmicks, his personality, connection and association, or organized programs. The visionary's purpose is what propels him on to discover his vision. And vision brings every person to his center of assignment, the center of his gift, and the center of favors needed to fulfill one's life. The nerve of a vision is the purpose it must fulfill.

Purpose is the reason for a vision. Hence, the true meaning of our vision is the identification of one's individual purpose, which manifests through his God-given activity. Like creating the waves, a visionary cannot create a vision but discovers it. It is God-created and God-given. And if the vision is God-centered through its creativity and allotment, then one can equally say that the key to applying the vision is directed by God.

Thus, a visionary like a sea surfer navigates on the sea waves and surfs to shore because he understands the movements of the waves. God gives us purpose in order for us to be purposeful. He also man-ifests the desire to fulfill the purpose, so that the purpose may be achieved. Vision is wired in our desires and through it, we search for the principles that make our vision realizable on earth. So, one must begin to understand that it is often not about ourselves in any way as we may think, but it is all about God.

In every generation, God blesses His own will, intentions, and purposes for that generation. All people do is to discover those intentions and purposes and fulfill them. The essence of all this is to show God's intentions and motives on mankind, whether as in vision, purpose, leadership, business entrepreneurship, entertainment, sports, among others. We recognize the workings of God and we join in His endeavors. This brings success and prosperity to man.

In other words, it takes the concerted effort of life's virtues such as faith, diligence, sincerity, focus, and persistence to discover the move of God and join in them. No true vision can be actualized without these forces stated above. May I point out that every individual is assigned with a definite purpose and so a healthy life begins around a visionary who has discovered his or her "in-Christ identity" and not a personal created identity.

In our bid to do something we do things probably outside of our assigned reasons for being humans. And failure is inevitable when we just do something for doing sake. So often, we end up as successful failures judged by our reason for existing. If you succeed in anything God did not assign you to do on earth, you're a successful failure. Your success can be described as bad success according to Joshua 1:8.

Visionaries don't create purposes and visions; they discover and live in them and apply themselves to the vision principles. This ensures effectiveness and efficiency; they do not just become busy people with one's own life. They tap into God and apply His wisdom and fulfill the vision, as it should be. Most often, visionaries have discovered their real-life identity and purposes on earth.

And when one understands the reason for one's life, then one can say, "I have a precise vision and I know exactly what I can do; I know what I cannot do. I know my business and what my business is not; I have limitations and I respect the boundaries of my limitations." And it is paramount to know that being a visionary is a natural part of our human makeup. However, thinking like a visionary is difficult because it is an attitude we must develop. It takes mental renewal and transformation from conformities of all types, including a servant mind-set to become a visionary and a leader.

Without any shadow of a doubt, a person who discovers his purpose is a genuine visionary and leader, and such a person exhibits unique qualities. It is admirable when one sees various expressions of vision traits in people with high-quality lifestyles. It shows how each of us should do something different but important to bring beauty to our glorious world.

In the next chapter, I have carefully researched and become convinced that every individual visionary displays diverse habit traits and my readers can equally discover their identity and purpose to paint their own portrait of vision, purpose, and leadership for effectiveness and efficiency.

Chapter 2

EXPRESSIONS OF VISION

There are visible signs in a grown up and likewise in a child. When you meet a grown up some of the visible signs on him show he's not a child. Beard, muscles, thought processing—all these are signs of growth and maturity. Everything has a characterized trait and it includes that of a visionary. When a person is walking in the positive power of vision, he portrays traits of vision.

The question is obvious, how can you see a person walking in the power of vision? The traits of vision can be demonstrated in so many ways and the strength of one's vision is seen in the purpose of the vision. Visionary leaders are successful people concentrated in their skill and purpose doing just one thing.

They're different from other people who may also be well-concentrated guys doing everything. The difference between a visionary and others is found in how they do things. Others do everything with their mental concentration, but visionaries do one thing with all of their mental concentration.

And if the vision doesn't serve a purpose, then it will abuse a purpose. In trying to do everything, most people abuse their assigned purpose in life. Yes, this is because God, the true vision giver, is diverse in nature and He expresses Himself in us through various channels to fulfill His purposes. We only concentrate in our discovered assignments and fulfill them. The world is divided into purpose fulfillers and purpose abusers and no man plays a neutral role. In reality and by our own known and unknown actions or inactions we fulfill or abuse purposes.

In this way, our responsibility as matured and experienced men is the capacity and recognition of our God-given traits as channels to reach our goals and dreams. Where an individual stands in God determines the kind of vision and purpose he may discover and pursue in his assigned life. As visionaries, we catch vision based on where we stand, and we attract people by who we are, not by who we want to be.

Our description and expression of our visions and purposes depend on the positions we assume. A story is told of four blind men who were asked to describe an elephant and based on where they stood they gave their respective versions of one big animal. All the four described one animal objectively different from the other. The mammal was one big thing but where they stood gave them a different description. God is bigger than the elephant, and where we stand around Him expresses our visions and purposes.

Humans and all creations generate the positive power of seeing the right source of our life revolving around God. And this source helps us to be highly effective people on earth. God created everything on earth for a purpose; both big and small and known and unknown things on earth all serve God's manifold purposes. Every creation has a source for living and survival through which it becomes effective on earth.

Each one of God's creations is created from its source and if it remains in the source, it functions effectively on earth. All creations must stay connected to their source to function, including seeing positively. The glories of God's creations are expressed through a connection to the source. All His creations when they die go back to their sources as ingredients for revitalization of the source. The more we are connected to our source the more power of positive sights, visions, and revelations we get in life as dominion agents. Our senses of elevation rise when we remain connected to our source of existence.

Therefore, no two people are the same and do the same things. They are different from each other, so they do different things. When we see two people do the same things it means one of them has lost his source; therefore, he or she is copying or duplicating. Two people may always have similar vision assignments, purposes, and leadership but they are always different in their application.

This is the true meaning of the principle of interdependency (where each relies on the other to progress), and which has its true origination from dependency and independency. The principle of dependency is the principle where we depend on somebody to identify our vision, purpose, and leadership. The principle of independence is the area of discovery of self in Christ, self-esteem, confidence, assignments, and purposes.

Let's consider this fact a very important platitude; this is an obvious remark anyway—vision declaration is God-given and men express it in a unique way. We express visions in the way we catch them, not the way we think about them. And hence, we must be responsible as skillful thinkers to demonstrate how to get our vision fulfilled. We must learn how to fulfill our respective visions in the dimensions of thoughts as we catch them. That is, we should cultivate the habit and ethics of asking the right questions.

In order to design the right strategic plans, the right questions should be designed around the plans. Solomon in Proverbs 18:13 (TLB) says, "What a shame—yes, how stupid!—to decide before knowing the facts!" Knowing facts and figures is the reason for asking the right questions for the vision. Designed questions like these are very crucial to help one succeed.

- How many people really discover their God-given, God-created visions? And, have I discovered mine?

- Do men actually wait for the right principles before they execute their visions? Am I a principled-based individual or a personality-based entity and anything goes?

- Why do some visionaries succeed and others fail? Where is my personal position in terms of my vision?

- Can one really say to himself, "What I am doing is what God has told me to do"?

- Why do some visionaries start up very well, but along the way they seem to stop growing, fall flat, and decline?

- Why do some visionaries struggle for many years, but when getting to the end they make it big to the top?

- What will one's likely visible and invisible obstacles be in his or her pursuit of vision? One should not consider his big dream and say, "Oh no, how can I achieve this? It's bigger than myself." If your dream is small, then you make God small. But if your dream is big, then you will make Him bigger than your big dreams.

The problem is the deficient societal tradition of low-level thinking. That is, thinking about dreaming small dreams, thinking small, and starting small; and that we must learn how to consider small things and never think too big of anything. Well, I differ. I have God, so I want to think the way He thinks and get it His way. God thinks very big as a big God of all so-called gods. Yet, He always begins every big thing He has ever done in a very small way. It is believed that a visionary can jump over every obstacle and win, starting in a very small way in life. He'll eventually get better and not bitter. In the subsequent chapters, I have dealt with how to overcome the obstacles in the way to discovering our visions.

Mostly, healthy growing, vibrant visions are always led by visionaries who have been there for a long period of time probing questions for better answers and solutions. They have been tested, tried, and proven. Their tenacities are constructed through various vicissitudes and tests. For example, they once fell in the oceans of the waters of life and were able to swim ashore after serious difficulties.

They have been likewise thrown into the furnace of fire, and instead of burning to ashes they had a chemical change and got refined and redefined. They fell into thick darkness but eventually saw the light of another day. They have climbed the high mountains and descended again as better and experienced individuals. The test of the valleys and gully experiences were obstacles that they once overcame.

Right and good questions also show our personal initiatives and they express how we demonstrate our assigned vision to influence society. Of course, the question we design and ask demonstrates the trait of expression we developed as visionaries.

For instance, the various understated traits are some of the many ways visionaries demonstrate vision. They do so through the use of the power of positive imagination, high sense of visualization, revelations, dreams, and goal setting; that is, strategic planning, innovation, self-cultivation, persistence, discipline, prioritization, synergy, passionate and maniacal desires, the powerful principles of assimilation and association, among others. An individual designs questions and displays the traits of vision for his purpose and leadership. So in this book and specifically in this chapter, I will discuss some of the traits, not trying to suggest that the rest is less important.

➤ Vision Is Seeing through the Power of Your Imagination

The positive power of imagination cannot be overemphasized. And it is possible when a person gets properly connected to his source of existence, to imagine fruitfully. After all, "Imagination rules the world" (Napoleon Bonaparte). One's imaginative faculties become infinitely functional anytime he stays connected to God, who is his true source of survival.

So then, he begins to think great and big to become global, instead of the normal small thinking people who are locals. Believe me, everyone is a total summation of his thinking and imagination. And that is why you must dare to dream bigger than yourself and never be afraid to have big dreams. The future of the world belongs to imaginative dreamers.

You will be left behind if you can't imagine and dream for the future. This is because every achiever is an imagination-oriented person. And all imagination-oriented persons are terminators of poverty circumstances and impossibilities in the world. Great "imagineers" don't have the words "can't" or "impossible" in their dictionaries and vocabularies.

To them, one should not say a statement like, "I can't." Rather, they express themselves this way, "How can I?" Instead of saying, "I'm impossible," they say, "I'm possible." Our imagination portrays or betrays us as creative or uncreative people depending on how we use them in the positions of life. High sense imaginative approach or low sense imaginative approach is an occurrence of one's own thinking faculty.

Uncreative imagination is unproductive and every kind of unproductive imagination is a wicked, destructive one. Any impossibility can be possible if you can imagine a breakthrough. Jesus said that all things are possible to them that believe (see Mark 9:23). And we can consider it the other way around—all things are impossible to them that believe so. Much as one's beliefs are possible, one's doubts are equally possible. Our doubts elevate impossible situations to rule over us. But our beliefs suppress and elevate possibilities to rule and reign in our own lives like kings and champions.

Matthew Ashimolowo, wrote in his book, *Be the Best* (2005), "One must think differently in order to succeed differently." It is believed that fortunes don't answer to fortunate people, they respond to the imaginative, wise men. Everything existed once upon a time as an image in our imagination, and the wise work desperately and bring their imaginations out by faith. It's our capacity to learn the rules of our vision elements that bring growth, establishments, and successes; not desires that increase a man's yens (earnings).

Inventors and all creative-minded people know the great secret of the power of human imagination. Good inventions or deeds are the absolute display of positive, imaginative thinking. Through the positive power of the human imagination, man has conquered space, the ocean, and the earth. And evil deeds that the world has experienced like the Holocaust, the Darfur genocide, the World Trade Center attacks (9/11) came from some individuals who permitted destructive beliefs in their minds.

There is power in focused imagination, so it is important that we learn how to master it. Focusing determines how we feel too. Our feelings are always put into action to determine the consequence of our actions. No one can determine the consequence of an action; we can only determine our actions. Therefore, it is very important for us to focus properly and feel right so that we avoid regrets and guilt as a result of the consequences of our actions.

What a person imagines is what comes to him. Frank Woolworth imagined himself selling outmoded items as a store clerk and using the same avenue to open chains of brilliant "Five Cent Stores" and ended up a billionaire. The power of positive imagination brought ordinary men to the limelight of glory and riches; Wilbur and Orville Wright, Henry Ford, Pelé, Roger Milla, Michael Schumacher, and Tiger Woods, as well as the world's richest man—Jeff Bezos—are all creative, imaginative thinkers.

Let imagination be the best or among the best in everything one does and it will become the best or one of the best tools for success. This is the secret of Lester Lewis, the great reggae maestro, and also of Shah Rukh Khan, the Indian film star who once said in an interview with CNN, "I always see myself as the best actor in the world and I achieved this amazing result." Therefore, we must build our imaginations in a multidimensional way as we learn how to focus on a thing one level at a time.

A person can easily change his destiny in no time if he dares to apply his imaginative skills. Focused imagination is the mind, which has been structured on a particular purpose through a particular vision for a particular accomplishment. Derailed imagination is the mind that has been persuaded to think other than what it is supposed to dream. Don't come to me and say, "I can't do anything," because you can do something. You can do anything you imagine if you can wait for it. The proof of one's patience is the ability to wait. He who resents waiting reveals his impatience.

Search yourself, search within and fish out that imaginative idea and you will be the best. One must see his or her capabilities and hidden skills, which often manifest themselves as a hobby. Apply yourself to the hobby you imagined and advertise it; soon you will become the CEO of your hobby and end up richer, if not the richest. Comprehensive, imaginative thinking breeds confidence as a reward.

On the other hand, incomprehensive imaginations breed vices, such as fear, intimidation, timidity, and inferiority complex. Any time one thinks rightly and acts appropriately, it shows one's imaginative ability and competence in a vision. This right act will yield the right consequences worthy of praise and emulation. The preservation of a person is seen in the vision that that person has.

The image one cultivates has a strong influence over the imagination that builds up in one's own mind. Poor self-image reflects in poor imaginative thinking and therefore poor acts. Good self-image reflects in good imaginative thinking and good acts. The revelation we have as individuals originates from the attitudes and principles of our deep sense of imaginations. The power of positive revelatory imaginations then becomes the mark of an excellent person.

I insist that a person must be bold to confront the negative things that fight his positive imaginations. I heard a preacher say to a congregation, "Be encouraged and crash your negative world with a powerful imaginative spirit." How right he was! As people of power, we have power over circumstance; we become effective people on earth when we learn how to deal with negative setbacks by right kingdom attitudes. Negative thinking is one of those setbacks that militate against our vision progress, and we can effectively deal with it through the Kingdom teachings of Apostle Paul in 2 Corinthians 10:3-6 (ASV):

> *For though we walk in the flesh, we do not war according to the flesh (for the weapons of our warfare are not of the flesh, but mighty before God to the casting down of strongholds); casting down imaginations, and every high thing that is exalted against the knowledge of God, and bringing every thought into captivity to the obedience of Christ; and being in readiness to avenge all disobedience, when your obedience shall be made full.*

➤ We Become Effective People When We Think and Act Correctly

God gave man a brain that makes him think and act correctly. When a man reasons properly it shows the impact of positive imagination, which equally goes further to fulfill the reason for his creation. The little brain cells form the huge dynamic component of the mind; yet, any individual who masters and engages the mind propels himself to the top. According to neurosurgeons, we may have to use less of our minds, probably just about 10 percent, to get hold of what we have been seeing. We must master how to engage our minds to utilize the created vision of our life.

We need to discover, know, and understand the vision itself and apply our minds to it. Then, we need to apply ourselves via time to properly use the right resources to get the vision accomplished. We must ride on the current of vision and surf as farther down the shore of achievements time and space offer. Note that building a vision wave is God-given but surfing on vision waves as the apparatus to the shore is man-made. Visionaries are surfers of vision waves and not creators of vision waves.

Hence, if one lives without thinking of how his discovered vision will win achievements, one will live below one's human mental capacity and expectation. He will be poor. Champions hardly weep in poverty, they only will to win and they win, no matter what because they know the secret of life's complexities and they apply their minds to think of a solution.

Instead of sitting down to complain as individual champions, they start to campaign to complete their winning mandates. The poorest person on earth is the one who refuses to engage his mind in a worthwhile thinking process. Your mental imagination is the unseen achievement waiting to be transmuted/translated/transported and duplicated in real-life circumstances. This makes humans successful and prime leading bosses in career skills.

➤ Vision Is Passionately Settling down on One's Imaginative Desire

One's desire to be different in life amongst other people makes him different. The desire to be or not to be is in our own hands and we control the diameter of our own circumferences within, which operate our lives. The quality of the desire we possess opens and shapes our lives and determines our placements in world affairs.

The visionary may not attract first-time persons; notwithstanding, he will always be the reason why people are attracted to them. The kind of desires that grow in an individual influence what kind of character ethics that individual displays and what kind of people he attracts. He is the main attraction because he is the vision carrier.

So, the visionary and his characteristics will buy him the world or he will sell himself uncooked and earn rejection in the world. The desire to think comprehensively and imagine appropriately also forms part of the vision confidence. The strong desire to create worthy imagination leads to the fulfillment of life's purposes. It also crafts and erects one's image in the public eye as a true leader. And when one desires and imagines properly, one has already achieved success. Oftentimes, people imagine negative things instead of positive things.

Our desires are so strong that they can captivate our emotions and feelings. Strong desire can render a person as a dogmatic (individual) entity. Strong desires motivate people to do things they would not do under normal circumstances. Human beings are more likely to attempt to do things they are convinced of strongly than to do things they are forced to do.

Therefore, I urge all to choose the right path and remain a fanatic, rather than to choose the wrong path and be dogmatic. How strong a person's desire is, shows how strong a person's action is. Strong action is evidence of a strong, passionate, or maniacal desire. Weak action is evidence of a person's weak desires. The principle of "positive seeing" is the direction by which each individual only wins when one's desires are strong, positive, and active toward a worthwhile goal.

What we desire is what we have done in the realm of the invisible. Let's, for instance, use the doctrinal teaching of Christ as a study case. Note that we are talking about getting what one desires in life. Jesus taught His disciples the sin of unlawful looking; that is, if you look at a woman and desire her in your heart, you have committed adultery already with her (see Matthew 5:28).

So in the eyes of God, adultery is not just the natural carnal and actual act of a physical, sexual offense, but also the thinking of the sexual offense in the mind. Therefore, it should be noted that the sexual offense takes place in the spiritual and invisible world and we replicate it in the world as a secondary phase of an act.

This same principle works in the school of positive desires and imaginations. For example, if a person desires a house, land, achievement, and success and he imagines he has it, he already possesses it. So then, the reality of what we do is not only what we see, but also what we think and imagine. Wow! The power and effect of positive desire are equal to positive achievement. What we see forms what we desire and imagine. And what we imagine finds its way to be duplicated in this material and tangible world.

It looks as if some invisible forces pull our desires from the realms of the unseen to the seen. Therefore, the ability and capacity to see what one desires become his "focus and all that he will amount to in life." The big image one sees represents the big image one gets. We are an encapsulation of our imaginations and desires.

Also, name any persons or a society whose people are optimistic, resolute, and absolutely positive and I will show you they were visionaries. Mention to me any nation that has experienced long-term prosperity and civilization and I will tell you where to find a people of pragmatic vision and a high degree of mental imaginations. Americans sent three astronauts in a spaceship that would ultimately land on the moon because they had President J. F. Kennedy who desired, tuned, and attuned their imagination toward such possibility in their time.

Vision, indeed, is that divine desire imagined by a person or group of people. The spirit of powerful desire, imagination, and self-styled visualization will break through every single impossible limitation in our way. Every "demon wall" shall fall flat when one sees, visualizes, desires, and imagines it broken.

As a visionary trying to set up a kingdom model in a tight Romanism systematic environment, I have discovered by experiential knowledge that there is never a breakthrough of any kind until there is a break.

For example, on October 14th, 1947, an air force pilot, Charles "Chuck" Yeager, broke the sound barrier because he saw himself fly a jet at the velocity speed over 750 miles per hour. Darryn Lyons, known in the famous world of photography as "Mr. Paparazzi," broke records and came to the celebrity world and success because of his strong desire to do so. He said to CNN in an interview, "We live in a century of celebrity obsession." We can also talk about Haile Gebrselassie from Ethiopia, who had a strong desire to conquer the world of mileages and marathons in sports. When he broke the world record, he came out with these words, "I told you that athletics is my life."

All these aforementioned changed their world in which they lived because they had an uncommon desire ignited by passion and enthusiasm. It is said that people who change the world started by first declaring independence from other people's expectations and becoming die hard for what they perceived to be their light and illumination. If you fear to make a declaration of independence, you cannot achieve self-government now nor in the near future.

Charles, Darryn, and Gebrselassie all cultivated a common trait of self-independence and a strong, passionate desire to break the barriers and limitations in their lives through the positive power of inherent desires and success passions. We can equally break every barrier in our lives if we see ourselves do it. We cannot afford to negate vision and suffer the consequence of failure and heartbreaks. Heartbreaks are inevitable conditions when there are no breakthroughs for the things we often desire or want to break.

It seems to me that the forces of cooperative desire in our imagination are too strong for the achievement of dreams and visions. What we see is what we desire and what we desire is what we imagine and what we imagine is what we think. What we think is what we believe and what we believe is what we do. The result of what we do is what we get. So from now on begin to: **see it, desire it, imagine it, think it, do it, and get it**.

And when we begin to see it, we will begin to think it, and when we begin to think it, we will also talk it. One must learn how to walk in the things one talks about and his own life will be fashioned the way he sees and imagines it. Respect in life is the ability to say what one means and says. Every true visionary has this key. A person's entire life begins to take the shape of what he sees and imagines every day. While "we cannot choose how many years we will live, we can choose how much life those years will have" (John C. Maxwell, *Developing the Leader Within You*, Thomas Nelson Inc. 1993).

I have for many years tried to get close to people who seem to be getting on well in life. A common phenomenon and a pattern are noticeable about all successful people. They always seem to desire and do something daily that the unsuccessful ones ignore and do once in their entire lifetime. They all seem to be very serious practicing and mastering their unseen thoughts and getting them established on paper and then on established tangible lands.

Brian O'Neil in the NBA, golf masters Tiger Woods and Vijay Singh, as well as all other celebrity sportsmen have strong desires to win and they dare do great visualization before they step out unto the field to conquer near-impossible challenges. So with these great attitudes, they get revered destinies. Don't ever forget this secret. Successful people do daily what unsuccessful people do once in a while. The secret of success or failure is discovered in human routines. You can never outwit your own habits or attitudinal ethics. See what you want and desire with passion and maniacal will and you can succeed appropriately.

➤ Vision Expresses Itself in Positive Visualization

No one is as strong or as weak as his own visualization. What one sees, concentrates on, and also visualizes, forms one's strengths or weaknesses. The account of Moses about the twelve spies is worthy of consideration. Numbers 13:33 (KJV) says, "And there we saw the giants, the sons of Anak, which come of the giants: and we were in our own sight as grasshoppers, and so we were in their sight."

The giants never reported their personal view about the spies. Instead, the spies generated their personal opinion of themselves as the view of the giants. A great lesson emerges here: that people see us based on how we see ourselves. Therefore, we must learn how to project the right images for public consumption. We must learn how to properly manage information so that the pictures we generate of ourselves (beings) will help facilitate our personal opinion in the light of God's view.

THE TYPE OF THE CITY OF BABEL

In Genesis 11:2-6, a revealing story also tells the laudable power of positive visualization. Seeing and imagining are paramount. In a visual reality, the famous tower of Babel teaches men a unique sense on the power of seeing and getting what we see. A story is told of a group of people, the Nimrod Cushite race, who spread from the families of Noah's descendants and journeyed from the East. They finally settled in the plains of Shinar and made a home there.

In principle, I believe that the first step in beginning an active, imaginative visualization is settling down somewhere. Find a convenient spot and settle down. Let's learn how to settle down with one skill, one business, and one project; let's complete one dream and move on to the next. We cannot achieve anything as people who do everything at the same time. Some people have wandered for far too long. They cannot settle down with one discipline of life. This is why some people are jack-of-all-trades and masters of none. Such people do everything in life and do none so excellently.

Once we ever emerge as the jacks-of-all-trades, we have equally signed a warrant to be labeled masters of none. Such people cannot receive anything of the Lord or of men. We must make a home for what we see and give birth to our dreams. Let's be positioned and see well into a visualized venture and go all out for it. This is what gave the electric bulb to the world. Thomas Edison settled down somewhere and visualized giving artificial light to the dark world. After many experiments, he got what he saw. Today the whole world is the beneficiary of magnificent colors of various electric bulbs due to Edison's vision.

And even as black people, we have little recorded versions of our achievements, in terms of participation and contribution to the scientific development of our modern world. We should not forget that "the skin has no place where the will is ripe to achieve heights" (Marfoh, LSK, News Africa; Year 6-No 5, May 2008). The history books recorded many opinions of others about us, not our personal opinions. If you don't write about yourself, your neighbor will and will describe you the way he wants. The world seems to believe in written stories more than verbal statements. Write your own story and tell the world about yourself.

So distortions, misinformation, and misinterpretations were used as powerful tools to subjugate, segregate, and marginalize our efforts as highly intelligent and recognized people, making us part of the compartmentalized Third World. Who cares? As people of color, we initiated, upgraded, and upheld the most unwanted abominations of all—idolatry. In this book, I have no intention to address such issues widely so we may have to drop it and pick it at the appropriate quarters. However, everywhere we go as people, we live to leave; we will take something home from where we go, and we will leave something good in the place we visited as we depart.

But the question is, who strategically purposed this misinterpretation that we did not participate and contribute to technology, as if we did not initiate any of these thought-provoking questions? I don't know either. Yet, we contributed significantly to all forms of human development in previous generations. But instead of writing the side of our stories, we rather left them in the hands of some people and this has become our bane. Hence, some of the views highlighted are not the exact things related to the black man. There has been mis-information as a result of misinterpretations of underlining facts. And this is because of enslavement and colonization. Our significant contributions in relation to inventions like that of Thomas Edison have been buried and not given the desired publicity. We actually participated in a great way to the technological advancement of the New World.

Quite recently, I read an article on our participation and no matter how humorous the writer appeared, I find it necessary to reproduce the entire write up for my readers to digest:

Life without black people

A very humorous and revealing story is told about a group of white people who were fed up with African Americans, so they joined together and wished themselves away. They passed through a deep dark tunnel and emerged in a sort of a twilight zone where there is an America without black people. At first these white people breathed a sigh of relief. At last, they said, No more crime, drugs, violence and welfare. All of the blacks have gone! Then suddenly, reality set in. The "NEW AMERICA" is not America at all—only a barren land.

1. *There are very few crops that have flourished because the nation was built on a slave-supported system.*

2. *There are no cities with tall skyscrapers because Alexander Mils, a blackman, invented the elevator, and without it, one finds great difficulty reaching higher floors.*

3. *There are few if any cars, because Richard Spikes, a black man, invented the automatic gearshift, Joseph Gambol, also black,*

invented the Super Charge System for Internal Combustion Engines, and Garrett A. Morgan, a black man, invented the traffic signals.

4. *Furthermore, one could not use the rapid transit system because its procurer was the electric trolley, which was invented by another black man, Albert R. Robinson.*

5. *Even if there were streets on which cars and a rapid transit system could operate, they were cluttered with paper because an African American, Charles Brooks, invented the street sweeper.*

6. *There were few if any newspapers, magazines and books because John Love invented the pencil sharpener, William Purveys invented the fountain pen, and Lee Barrage invented the Type Writing Machine and W. A. Love invented the Advanced Printing Press. They were all, you guessed it, Black.*

7. *Even if Americans could write their letters, articles and books, they would not have been transported by mail because William Barry invented the Postmarking and Cancelling Machine, William Purveys invented the Hand Stamp and Philip Downing invented the Letter Drop.*

8. *The lawns were brown and wilted because Joseph Smith invented the Lawn Sprinkler and John Burr the Lawn Mower.*

9. *When they entered their homes, they found them to be poorly ventilated and poorly heated. You see, Frederick Jones invented the Air Conditioner and Alice Parker the Heating Furnace. Their homes were also dim. But of course, Lewis Lattimer later invented the Electric Lamp, Michael Harvey invented the lantern, and Granville T. Woods invented the Automatic Cut off Switch. Their homes were also filthy because Thomas W. Steward invented the Mop and Lloyd P. Ray the Dust Pan.*

10. *Their children met them at the door—barefooted, shabby, motley and unkempt. But what could one expect? Jan E. Matzelinger invented the Shoe Lasting Machine, Walter Sammons*

invented the Comb, Sarah Boone invented the Ironing Board, and George T. Samon invented the Clothes Dryer.

11. *Finally, they were resigned to at least have dinner amidst all of this turmoil. But here again, the food had spoiled because another Black Man, John Standard invented the refrigerator.*

Now, isn't that something? What would this country be like without the contributions of Blacks, as African-Americans?

Martin Luther King, Jr. said, "by the time we leave for work, Americans have depended on the inventions from the minds of Blacks."

Black history includes more than just slavery, Frederick Douglass, Martin Luther King, Jr., Malcolm X, and Marcus Garvey & W.E.B Dubois.

—Tony Koki, 2007
Courtesy of modernghana.com
PLEASE SHARE ABUNDANTLY

Tiger Woods settled in the village of golf and visualized himself as the best or one of the best players, and he has become the king of the game. Larry King visualized interviewing every star on earth, and he is still doing it after many years of admirable journalism successes. In Italy, for example, a Ghanaian by the name of George Henry Wood visualized himself as the New Age immigrant factory lord, and today he is cutting and molding glass windows in his own factory in the city of Brescia.

Mario Barwuah Balotelli, born in Italy from Ghanaian parents, settled down and visualized himself as a football star, and today he is playing as a top footballer in Europe with the elite sides. Consider the former heavyweight champion Evander Holyfield. He knocked down "Iron" Mike Tyson (the undisputed champion of the ring) in his heydays. Evander said, "I saw myself knock him down"; suggesting he visualized and defeated the undefeated champion.

Booker T. Washington is known in history as the first African American to have engaged in reading and writing. He could do that by overcoming many imposed odds and difficulties. The key to his success was the spirit of positive visualization—we get whatever we see in life if we can commit our passion, skill, and life to it.

Nothing is impossible to what the eye sees. He hid himself and learned how to read and write. His sense of imagination saw reading and writing as a basic skill necessary for his progress out of segregation, racism, imposed marginalization, and humiliation, which were not powerful enough as external factors to quench his desire to achieve the skills of reading and writing.

A champion visualizes and gets what he sees. Learning how to think and visualizing straight equally means learning how to avoid waywardness in our minds because we move and build direction from our most dominant thoughts. If we want to break through in the area of desire, our thinking should be right.

Let's go back to Babel and then learn from the citizens of the Shinar plains that caught a vision. They saw and visualized the plains turned into an urban city with a skyscraper as the center of attraction. And they immediately got what they saw and imagined. Did they really get it? Yes, they did; because once it's thought of, imagined, and visualized, it already exists. You only wait for the physical manifestation to occur. You wait to transfer the first created thought thing to a second created physical thing.

The problem of mankind is not where the difficulties are positioned but what and how they visualize or see from where these are located. Quoting from the Scriptures (Genesis 11:3-4), "Then they said to one another, 'Come, let us make bricks and bake them thoroughly.' They had brick for stone, and they had asphalt for mortar... 'Come, let us build ourselves a city, and a tower whose top is in the heavens; let us make a name for ourselves, lest we be scattered abroad over the face of the whole earth.'"

Please take note of the motives for development. **One:** "Lest we be scattered abroad over the face of the whole earth." They did not want to see the same problem happen again that befell them as a result of the journey to the plains of Shinar; they were a mild-thinking, solution-minded group of people who hated to be wild-nomadic or seminomadic. They thought and visualized well, deviating from their past stories as wanderers. They visualized and offered a solution to the problem of Genesis chapter 10 in the Bible where families just split and segregated from each other.

Two: "Let us make a name for ourselves"; they visualized getting fame out of the desired achievement and also attracting the wealth of other nations for their nation. This means they saw and visualized themselves as super achievers. Making a name was not a big problem per se. After all, we saw in Genesis 12 that God promised Abraham a great name upon the earth. God Himself is the most famous being on earth. The fame of Christ spreads to the whole world. And also, His fame and doctrine convict people all over the continents of the earth and they are getting converted to the principal theology of a young Jewish rabbi who didn't travel abroad.

Fame then is not sinful as such. But the pride of fame destroys humans faster than the other known factors. As visionaries, we must know that three things are destructive—girls, gold, and glory. In other words, women, wealth, and the world can be destructive. We should, therefore, know that the most dangerous of the three destructive elements are the world and pride (see 1 John 2:15-16).

Jesus was very famous. And we can also be very famous. Everyone knows this basic truth and we all admire His fame. You can be known and admired too. The pride and arrogance of fame are sinful. The problem of Babel was that they attached self, that is, pride (self-glory), to their famous visualized desires and imagination and God saw haughtiness and arrogance in them. And that was bad because as Scripture says, "God resists the proud, But gives grace to the humble" (James 4:6b; 1 Peter 5:5c). The evil seed of arrogance has eaten deep into the moral fabric of man's heart so that he has become self-centered and self-conceited. The thoughts, "I, my, and me," are the root of self-ishness, which often rejects the mandate of God over a people.

Three: They visualized "a tower whose top [headquarters, authority, and instruction] is in the heavens." And this is where they missed it all. Remember, the urban skyline was not a problem to God, but the motive behind its development. The tower was a problem for God. The tower became the security and eyes of the people instead of God. They then took instructions and listened from the edit that came from the tower and therefore, it was a rejection of the sovereignty of God over their existence.

Also, remember that the devil had rebelled against God earlier with the same issue saying, "I will ascend into heaven…I will be like the Most High" (Isaiah 14:13-14). And he was able to persuade one-third of the angelic beings including man on earth to rebel against God. He sowed the seeds of rebellion and pride in man so that we yearned to occupy positions in the Heavens where God appointed His selected representatives.

However, consider what God said about the imaginative visualization of the people building the Tower of Babel. Genesis 11:6 says, "And the LORD said, 'Indeed the people are one and they all have one language, and this is what they begin to do; now nothing that they propose to do will be withheld from them.'" It was as if God was saying, "Behold the people is one, AND NOTHING CAN STOP THEM FROM GETTING WHAT THEY SEE."

Once a person has the desired picture within his heart, it cannot stay in there. It has to manifest itself. This is because anything you see is what you get. And the kind of gift a person gets reveals the vision that will also grow in him. So then, I urge people to see and get what they visualize or dream. Stephen R. Covey, a writer, once said, "Dreaming builds creative imagination. Then test your dreams. Are they based on principles? Are you willing to pay the price to achieve them?"

Leaders are visionaries whose purposes, among other things, are to engage in visualizations of all kinds. The secret for leadership is the positive power of seeing, even in the midst of difficulties.

➤ Vision Is the Positive Response and Absolute Adherence to Universal Principles and Laws That Govern Our Existence

"We are not laws unto ourselves, and the more we begin to value principles and people, the greater will be our peace," says Stephen R. Covey in *First Things First* (Free Press, 1994).

Principles are not values. Some bad boys can hold a common value system, which will fundamentally violate the basic principles and rules of life. Principles have eternal keys and they unlock every door in every generation. Methods vary daily depending on the skills we engage in. But principles are the foundations for methods to thrive. The more closely our paradigm of operation aligns with these principles, the more accurate and correct we are.

The undeniable fact is that life is centered and governed by laws. Traffic laws regulate our roads. Our nations and governments are all governed by systematic laws—scientific, religious, legal, legislative, executive, judicial, among others. The direction we take and whether we win or lose is determined by how effectively or ineffectively we understand the application of certain laws.

People often ask wrong questions in life related to their vision principles. The popular wrong question people often ask is this, "What will make this vision workable and accomplishable?" The unpopular right question should be, "What is preventing this vision from being achieved and accomplished?" When a person knows what prevents his fulfillment, he begins to discipline himself and averts the obstacle that obstructs him.

Laws govern every vision God helps us to discover. We discover every vision with related instructive laws to make things workable in society. When one gets a vision, he should wait and get the laws that govern and regulate the vision. Most often, the error of the "hyper quick-fix" individual is the speed he takes when a vision is apparent.

Every God-created, God-given, human-discovered vision is a living organism; and it will only grow by the right basic principle, which is to have the basic nutrients and be in the right environment. There is the paradigm potential principle: the idea that we are embryonic and we can grow and grow again and again in our talents, gifts, and knowledge. When the vision is not growing, something terrible might have happened; either there is an unhealthy situation around it, or the basic feeding systems lack nutrition.

Every living organism grows; we don't train them to grow. It is a natural phenomenon to see a child grow from childhood to adulthood if the right nutrients are supplied. We needn't command the young to grow. We supply them with the needed nutritional requirements, and they grow. What hampers and hinders growth may be poor nutrition, unsafe environments, and lack of proper childcare facilities. But when all these hindrances are removed, the child grows automatically.

In our argument, the vision is a living organism, just like the child. We as visionaries remove unwholesome hindrances and the cells of the organism multiply and flourish. The vision flourishes and blossoms in the visionary's individual design, which is as true of humans just as it is of nature. The vision cells blossom distinctively and the vision grows and fulfills its destined glory because the impending dangers are removed. The glory of the vision is the end result it produces, different from the more than six billion known visionaries on the earth planet.

How then can one remove the roadblocks of one's vision? This question is paramount. We need to erect efficient and effective timely universal principles for every God-centered vision. The key issue now is not just the existence of a vision, but the existence of healthy principles erected, based on time-tested principles and laws. Every God-centered thing has an explanation by a set principle, which helps give order to the thing to the end.

How these principles will work depends on how we understand and apply them. The implication of a principle or law is the application of the said law and vice versa. The realities of principles—spiritual, natural, and human—are obvious to each person as he thinks and tests the cycle and sees that time and time again the level of peace in man is related to the laws that move for either survival or stability, for disintegration or integration, for destruction or resolution. A principle-based visionary expresses his vision by predominant laws.

➤ Every Visionary Can Function Synergically to Express His Vision

Synergy may be defined as the ability and capacity for people with skill, intelligence, and directional knowledge to coordinate agreed efforts as a single unified force and mechanism by which their respective God-given, Christ-centered purposes will be accomplished without breaching on other people's liberties or freedoms.

Today, it is difficult for a lone ranger to be successful, even if it'll be a prototype gladiator game. In the film *Gladiator*, Russell Crowe, who played the protagonist, and his friends synergically defeated their enemies in the grand Colosseum in Rome; none could single handily do so. I believe that synergy puts human brains together as a single force for human accomplishments that supersedes single strength. Banks are coming together. Companies are emerging for power and supremacy in the world of business. Countries are coming together to gain ascendancy in world affairs. So, tell me who wants to go solo and I will point out to you the person who is failing.

The principles of synergy are rooted deep in our design where the legs characteristically walk, the hands take, the eyes see, the brain thinks, the heart conceives and perceives, and the tongue tastes and talks. We see synergic elements as the head carries the brain and more. Nature teaches deep principal lessons on synergy—the power of the school of fishes, the flying heights of a flock of birds, the team of antelopes or bulls, the pride of lions. So, why can't we also come together with a unified mind?

It's now a synergic world and not an energetic world. It is no more how powerful and effective we may be single-handedly but how effective, efficient, and powerful we have become in our corporate endeavors. Our world today is more of inspiration and less of energetic perspiration of muscles. When fools come together, they are stronger than a wise man. So, why should wise men not come together and be supermen? This is the principal key to leadership.

As visionaries, we express the spirit of synergy and confront our modern challenges. Though we may be the cutting-edge of the vision, we cannot be the rod. We may be the trigger, not the bullet. Coming together is a powerful force government's fear. When people get together, they become a stronger voice that must be listened to even if what they have to say is foolish. Continents like the Americas and Europe are strategically forming themselves into synergized groups in order to entrench their lead in world affairs. The United States of America and the European Union express unity and synergy for supremacy.

The purpose of synergy must be for the dominance and supremacy over creation, not over mankind. We cannot be dominant and supreme when we go all out but alone; we will be crushed to death. Synergy is not quantitative but qualitative. Numbers are not as important as cohesion and agreement in a worthwhile God-centered purpose.

In the apartheid era, 5 million white South Africans ruled and mesmerized 27 million black South Africans. The secret of dominance was in their synergized systematic structure, which was defensive and could not be penetrated. I believe that as humans we should master efforts to dominate creation and not ourselves. Therefore, any form of oppression, suppression, and dominance over one another should not be encouraged.

GOD IS SYNERGISTIC IN CHARACTER

Even God is synergic. He is the Godhead, a component of Father, Son, and Holy Spirit. In Moses's creative narratives we see the synergic moves of the Godhead Trinity (see Genesis 1:1-3). The effort of Heaven is always a synergic move in its entirety. God never walks and works alone; so men who are in the likeness and image of God should not walk and work alone. When He came to the Garden of Eden, we saw the presence of cherubim and a host of other heavenly elements (see Genesis 3:8, 23-24). Isn't synergy at work?

The dispensation of God is a component of the Father, the Son, and the Holy Spirit. The Bible can be divided into three relative dispensations: from Genesis to Malachi, from Matthew to Acts 1, and from Acts 2 to Revelation. The first dispensation was the direct ministry of the Father. The second dispensation was the ministry of the Son, and the third and last is the ministry of the Holy Spirit.

ABRAHAM, ISAAC, AND JACOB ARE A SYNERGIC REFERENCE

The highest-ranking spiritual men are also synergically interplayed. These three names—Abraham, Isaac, and Jacob—symbolize the highest spiritual authority and rankings in the relationship between man and God. God again has always introduced Himself to the people in synergic reference when it comes to the order of names (see Exodus 4:5).

› The Dynamics of Revelation in the Elevated Sense of Seeing

It is clear that everything is purposeful if we can see its revelation. Known or unknown, every created object of God has a purpose. The dynamics of revelation are seen in the elevation of the visionary. Revelation is the ingredient that throws an uncommon light on something and gives one a basic interpretation that elevates him to uncommon heights of blessings and breakthroughs. There is something to be revealed on everything, every person, and every circumstance on earth.

One must, therefore, seek it out and he will be elevated. God reveals things to people who fear Him and you can be one of them. He reveals them by the presence of the Holy Spirit in our lives.

It is then a mystery, which we take beneficial glory from when revelation comes to the soul. So, it is revealed and we humans, the kings of the earth, see the floodgates of glory. A wise Jewish rabbi had this to say on the positive power of revelation and elevated thinking,

> *Woe unto those who see nothing but simple narratives. Every word of scripture contains an elevated sense of hidden mystery. Every word has an elevated message to it; which is either a natural or an elevated mystery. The narratives of the scriptures are but a remnant in which the mysteries are closed or hidden. Do not mistake the remnant for the mysteries it contains.*

For now, I will conclude on the traits and expressions of visionaries. However, the basic fact remains that all visionaries express one or more of the traits inherent in visionaries.

Chapter 3

THREE LAWS THAT GOVERN SIGHT

Laws or principles govern life and not logics and personalities. And when one steps up and begins to act on his vision laws, it stirs up those around him to see and assist in the very thing they might have hindered. The fundamental adherence to the basic laws or principles in life leads to a smooth running of human affairs, the earth, and our environs. And the opposite is as true as possible: the lack of adherence to laws and principles in life leads to the degradation and destruction of our societal fabric, humans, and the earth as a whole.

Everything is a law in itself and also has a law or a principle that governs its external operation. Though everything is a law in itself, nothing is a law to itself. Nobody can ever be a law to himself. Everything should abide by external laws and principles. Our own successes in life are structured on how best we can recognize, obey, and adhere to known and unknown laws or the fundamental set of principles in one's environment.

God certainly rules in the affairs of men (see Daniel 5:21). But God governs the affairs of men through three basic principles on earth—spiritual, natural, and man-made. God made every law discovered in every field and discipline. And we should search out those laws and use them to enhance our lives on earth. More often than not, our ignorance in the operation of the basic laws of life has rendered us inefficient and ineffective.

One basic and important law is the principle of sight. Every motion has a related dynamic law and visionaries search to gain knowledge and understanding of the primary law that governs that particular motion. Don't ever move because something is moving. Study the dynamics of the laws that govern that movement and tap into it.

The ability to see and understand what is revealed and adapt to the foundational law that governs it generates success. Success is not cheap but a "chip." And if we know how to fix the "principle chip" in the right place, our life's machine revolves and makes a quick revolution at an indescribable velocity. Vision operates in the categorical laws that govern sight. But what is sight?

SIGHT

The *Collins Concise Dictionary: 21st Century Edition* has over 19 synonymous definitions for the word sight, among them are: "to aim using the sight, the power and faculty of seeing, the act or instance of seeing, the range of vision, anything that is seen and worth seeing, any of the various devices used to assist the eye in making alignment or directional observation."

There are three eyes and three sights of the body, and they are all as effective and beneficial. We have the eye of the spirit (spirit's eyes), the eye of the soul (soul's eyes), and the eye of the flesh (outer window of the body), which is fleshy and visible. The uses of our three sights depend on the individual's position in knowledge and understanding of those principles that govern them. When you acquire an elevated sense and revelation, you see with your spiritual eyes and get better. This is because one ceases to operate them from human thoughts and ways, to God's thoughts and ways.

The saddest curse on mankind is the capacity to see with the natural eyes but never perceive or understand with the inner eyes. And how one sees is defined by who one spends his or her quality time with. Therefore, it is very important that we choose friends who are going in the same direction as we are.

We must learn how to spend quality and positive time with people who influence us positively. One's time with a person of vision will help increase one's understanding on the major philosophy, discipline, and the kind of character that exhibits progress and vision success. Else, our own friends can become impediments and obstacles along the journey.

Jesus came to the earth so that men would discover themselves in God, their true source, and exercise their eyes in the three dimensions. He knew the secret of friendship, so He selected those ones who did not oppose His views, except the son of perdition. Remember, there has been no visionary as Christ Jesus and we have the mandate to look to Him from the beginning to the end (see Hebrews 12:2). Mary, the mother of Jesus, illustrates a detailed reflection on association and vision. When the angel of the Lord informed her of Elizabeth's pregnancy, she immediately traveled and associated with her for three months because she was also pregnant (see Luke 1:38-42).

Sight as a virtue, whether it is spiritual or natural, follows a designed pattern and a visionary cannot negate or push aside and succeed. Those who operate in the natural and soul-elevated senses (even when they learn the Scriptures) become scholastic intellectuals. Yet, they can operate from the highest human capacity covering, which is always inadequate to tap into the supernatural realm of God's Spirit. Jesus asked the disciples of John to go their way and tell him what they had seen (see Luke 7:22-26 KJV below):

Then Jesus answering said unto them, Go your way, and tell John what things ye have seen and heard; how that the blind see, the lame walk, the lepers are cleansed, the deaf hear, the dead are raised, to the poor the gospel is preached. And blessed is he, whosoever shall not be offended in me. And when the messengers of John were departed, he began to speak unto the people concerning John, What went ye out into the wilderness for to see? A reed shaken with the wind? But what went ye out for to see? A man clothed in soft raiment? Behold, they which are gorgeously apparelled, and live delicately, are in kings' courts. But what went ye out for to see? A prophet? Yea, I say unto you, and much more than a prophet.

In this direction, Jesus was shifting the mindset of His audience from human culture, carnal judgments, and world assessment to the spiritual-elevated truth of the Kingdom. Yes, in the natural sense you know kings must be posh. I am a king, yet I operate from low places and not palaces. In the spirit sense of spiritual elevation, you don't need to be in a palace to be recognized as a king.

You need to fulfill purpose assignment and kingdom mandate to be recognized and celebrated as a king. And even John may be considered a reed (weakling) tossed down to destruction by Herod's political edicts (doctrines). However, this man is more than a prophet. Among those born of women, there is not a greater prophet than John (see Matthew 11:11a; Luke 7:28a). But if my audience will believe and commit themselves to the Kingdom of God (their true source of life) the least among you shall be greater than John (see Matthew 11:11; Luke 7:28). Jesus came to lift man to a higher revelatory level.

OUR SOURCE DETERMINES AND INFLUENCES HOW WE SEE

How resourceful we become is based on how source oriented we are. It is vital to know and understand what the word source means. A spring that forms the starting point of a thing is the source. Source is the origination; it is where a person, circumstance, or a thing emanates, and it also determines how the person, circumstance, and thing will see and function among other reasons such as:

1. To have fellowship with the Father of light and exercise dominion on earth.

2. To discover and fulfill our purposes.

3. To release our lives' potentials into our purpose assignments.

4. To be fruitful and productive toward prosperity on earth.

5. To live and operate our lives in the material world as spirit beings via the elevated revelation of the written Word of God.

Without a proper connection to our source, we can't see well and survive the harsh climatic environment posed in life. Position is not as crucial and sensitive a subject matter as where we are coming from; that is, our true origination. Why? Because where we originate from dictates and determines the position we must occupy in life and what we must do and mustn't do in our positions.

Some of us in life have successfully occupied certain positions, but in principle, we may not be in our original mandated kingdom-assigned position, which is the main reason for our call and intended purpose. We have not discovered and defined our original God-given plan, so we are successful failures. We are operating in places God did not design for us on earth.

So we are carbon copies and duplicates of an original and are not worth a dime in our intended market price. If we had discovered ourselves, it would have been different. We must know that every single thing in life has a reason for being (purpose), a generation (time), a set order to follow (principle), and where to play (live and function).

Nothing exists for existence sake. If something does not exist in its chosen and selected parameter, it must exit. For example, as fallen human beings we have our roots in Hell or Heaven based on our own choice and will. So if a person refuses Christ's redemption, such source of living is associated with Satan. A person in Satan cannot produce righteousness. So, based on where he is coming from we know the type of thing such an individual will exhibit.

When we know where we come from, we also know what we must do. And aberrations will be reduced in our actions. Straightforwardness is evidence of pure direction and as we are tapped in our source we exhibit these traits. Our source of living dictates what we must do and we don't dictate to it what we want to do. Humans, as far as their purposes articulate in the principle of source, are called into absolute "zombisms" and nothing derails the mind from going any other way, but in its purpose assignments.

For instance, the bird flies because it has been designed from its source with the characteristics and potential of flight. The fish swims because it was designed by the principle of dynamic existence with the characteristics and potential for swimming. The bird flies and sees the way God designed it to see. The fish swims and sees as providence designed it. The bird sees in the air and the fish also sees in water. They all see because they are connected to their source of livelihood.

The fish or the bird never struggle to do what God designed them for. The potential in them helps them to fulfill their assigned purpose without training. We may have visions and be visionaries, we may have purposes and be very purposeful, we may be leading and be in leadership, but when we do all these in positions not meant for us, we become failures since we will not see how we ought to see.

Put the bird in water and it will surely suffocate and die within seconds. By the principle of dynamic existence, some birds can adventure in waters for their preys, but they can't remain in the water for their existence. In the same way, take the fish out of the water and it will die. A thing dies when it is disconnected from the source.

So once each one of the above maintains its position and assumes their respective God-given terra and responsibilities, they see from the perspective of their Maker. Their assignment helps them to see and their sight helps them to fulfill their assignment. This explains why the eagle, king of the birds, can fly thousands of feet in the skies and identify a mouse on the earth. The fish is centered in the waters, so it sees and swims from continent to continent and fulfills its assigned purposes.

The position of one's source defines and determines how one sees. For example, when humans are up in the skies above 33 thousand feet, houses appear like ants to them, unlike the eagle. We know we have conquered heights and space because we are the rulers of the earth, but we also know that we cannot live and survive in the air because that is not where we are suited to live since there will be no place to hang. That is not our place though we have the power to master the earth. So, where is our source? It is in the original position where our eyes function in the beautiful act of seeing.

EVERYTHING HAS A SOURCE

Everything has a source by which it displays its glory. The source of the fish and all aquatic creatures is the water (see Genesis 1:20-23 KJV below):

And God said, Let the waters bring forth abundantly the moving creature that hath life, and fowl that may fly above the earth in the open firmament of heaven. And God created great whales, and every living creature that moveth, which the waters brought forth abundantly, after their kind, and every winged fowl after his kind: and God saw that it was good. And God blessed them, saying, Be fruitful, and multiply, and fill the waters in the seas, and let fowl multiply in the earth. And the evening and the morning were the fifth day.

The source of the tree is the earth. Genesis 1:11-12 (KJV) say, "And God said, Let the earth bring forth grass, the herb yielding seed, and the fruit tree yielding fruit after his kind, whose seed is in itself, upon the earth: and it was so. And the earth brought forth grass, and herb yielding seed after his kind, and the tree yielding fruit, whose seed was in itself, after his kind: and God saw that it was good."

The source of all kinds of animals is also the same soil. Genesis 1:24-25 (KJV) say, "And God said, Let the earth bring forth the living creature after his kind, cattle, and creeping thing, and beast of the earth after his kind: and it was so. And God made the beast of the earth after his kind, and cattle after their kind, and every thing that creepeth upon the earth after his kind: and God saw that it was good."

If you remove any of these creatures from their source they die. This is because they will be sourceless and they cannot connect to their source for dynamic existence and survival. We are attached to our source to survive. Any creation that gets detached from the source dies. The plant withers away and it is only best for a fire when it is detached from the soil. The bird can't fly if it doesn't settle on the earth to eat. The fish will die when it is taken out of the water. None of these creatures will ever see and survive unless they remain in their sources of existence. This is a dynamic principle, the huge dynamic law of existence and survival.

MAN HAS A DUAL SOURCE

Genesis 1:26-28 and 2:5-8 define our sources. Genesis 1:26-28a (KJV) say, "And God said, Let us make man in our image, after our likeness… So God created man in his own image, in the image of God created he him; male and female created he them. And God blessed them."

Genesis 9:6b (KJV) reinforces 1:26 and 28: "For in the image of God made he man."

John 4:24 (KJV) explains what being the image and likeness of God means: "God is a Spirit." And so man is a spirit too because man came out of God. Then, the true source of man is in God. Man is connected to God as the spiritual source of his dynamic existence and nothing whatsoever can replace it. Genesis 2:5b-8 (KJV) say,

For the LORD God had not caused it to rain upon the earth, and there was not a man to till the ground. But there went up a mist from the earth, and watered the whole face of the ground. And the LORD God formed man of the dust of the ground, and breathed into his nostrils the breath of life; and man became a living soul. And the LORD God planted a garden eastward in Eden; and there he put the man whom he had formed.

HOW THE THREE LAWS OF SIGHT OPERATE IN OUR LIVES

We always look at a thing and then we see through the thing. We see and it is revealed. What one watches (as he looks) determines what shall be seen and revealed. So, it is first looking, second watching, and third seeing the revealed. We can only be elevated by what is seen and revealed.

Nevertheless, the purpose of revelation is to bring revival, revolution, and elevation. The huge dynamics that go with revelation are our willingness to respond to the laws of revelation and this book offers that. When we learn and master the basic laws that govern sight, we pair ourselves in the reality of revelation. In Ezekiel 40:4 (KJV), we see the three fundamental laws: "And the man said unto me, Son of man, behold with thine eyes, and hear with thine ears, and set thine heart upon all that I shall shew thee; for to the intent that I might shew them unto thee art thou brought hither: declare all that thou seest to the house of Israel." These laws are:

1. The first law is from the primary source, looking or "behold with thine eyes." The word "behold" is the common expression in our modern terminology which could mean look.

2. The second law is from the intermediate source, watching: "declare all that thou seest." Seeing then goes beyond just the casual art of looking. You first look at things and watch them closely in order to see into them. When it is seen, it is no more mere seeing, but that which has been revealed. This is one's ability to give identification, the capacity to grasp and recognize. In this case, it is a virtue to notice and witness in vivid understanding what it means and how it applies.

3. The third law is revelatory and most resourceful: "set thine heart upon all." This is in the elevated realm and the senses one receives within the spirit may not have anything to do with the natural eyes. God wants each person to get the spirit of revelation because He wants to elevate all of us on earth as dominion people.

Primarily, all humans have the ability to look at things within the parameters of their source. But this act does not guarantee seeing; it potentially guarantees seeing. And when we see based on where we stand, assigned principles and importance shall be revealed to us. It is upon the spirit of revelation and elevation that we take dominion as dominion agents.

So Apostle John should be on the Patmos Island to get revelation and elevation to the spirit times of the future generations way ahead of him. What you see determines what is revealed. Not everything we look at is that which we see into, and it is not everything we see that is revealed. Take your time from today. Look at things so carefully and closely.

Then watch what you fix your eyes on; you'll discover that you'll begin to see into it. Seeing is a gift in the revealed order of life. Seeing is the ability or capability, or otherwise, the capacity to make things out and discern their active presence in a condition and how to use these given opportunities to affect changes in any circumstance.

The fact that we looked did not ensure we saw. Most people look at things but they don't see them. Anytime one sees, personal experience (vital for individual progress) will be born: understanding will be thrown to your person, insight will be obtained, and finally, happiness will be your expression. This comes about because seeing develops the revelation needed for our private development and our personal enhancement in the knowledge of God. Before we expressed statements like, "I see," we first looked.

So, looking at things in a fantastic manner serves the first degree in the law of sight and seeing serves the second degree. The third degree is reflective and it is in the soulful and spiritual revelatory realm. Normally, at this juncture, our human senses count little because they are dormant and docile. This kind is a perception in either our heart or the spirit of the mind. This type of seeing has nothing to do with the natural ability of the eyes. That is why Helen Keller, who was born blind, deaf, and dumb, rose in life and became a star traveling the world over and teaching and motivating people to see and change their lives' circumstances. She said the greatest woe of man is to have natural eyes and yet see nothing.

Seeing is always a spirit-to-spirit communication, and only those who have their natural senses inactive or dead, or for that matter, spiritual senses active operate in this realm. Paul said that the Spirit (of God) bears witness with our spirit (human spirit) that we are the children of God (see Romans 8:16). As believers, we must be informed about our position in communication. Spirits communicate with spirits, souls to souls, and flesh to flesh.

In the spirit, we see and get revelations to compare spiritual things with the spiritual (see 1 Corinthians 2:13). Of course, "Eye hath not seen, nor ear heard, neither have entered into the heart of man, the things which God hath prepared for them that love him" (1 Corinthians 2:9 KJV).

Both first and second-degree sight fall short of grasping spiritual realities. God has revealed spiritual realities only through spirit-to-spirit communication. Deep spiritual realities are revealed to the believer who operates from the spiritual sense.

The Greeks call such functioning *rhema*. If one operates on the plains of first and second-degree sight, he moves in the dimension of *logos*. Yet, Jesus taught His disciples about the written logos or written word as dead and it profits nothing. Rather, the spirit profits and gives life to us (see John 6:63).

Paul admonishes that we should henceforth know everything after the order of the spirit of revelation: "Wherefore henceforth know we no man [including Jesus] after the flesh: yea, though we have known Christ after the flesh, yet now henceforth know we him no more" (2 Corinthians 5:16 KJV). So it is irrelevant to keep the embalmed remains of a dead person. It is a form of dynamic new age idolatry and sacrilege, an abomination punishable by the judges. This is because the latter (material) kills but the spirit gives life.

This also means that anything a person looks at and sees has a spiritual implication, which is more important than the natural implication. A spiritual man should look at a thing and see the revelation of the mysteries of the Kingdom. Whatever we look at and see must lead us to the revelation of the spirit and give us the implicative and applicative sense of the spiritual.

Consider Jeremiah 1:11-12 (KJV): "Moreover the word of the LORD came unto me, saying, Jeremiah, what seest thou? And I said, **I see a rod of an almond tree**. Then said the LORD unto me, Thou hast well seen:

for I will hasten my word to perform it." In other words, the Lord is saying, "Jeremiah, I have shown an almond tree and it implies My Word and how fast I am at performing what I say."

SYMBOLISM OF TREE

The word tree in the Bible means a lot. Never read the Scriptures and confine definitions of plurality to interpretation. There are always other meanings waiting to express themselves if you develop your mind to become a breeding ground for God's blessings. Where it manifests indicates what it means. We may probably have to look at a few of those examples as are available now and use this as a guide in our subsequent interpretation of spiritual truth when necessary. For instance, in Genesis, a tree symbolically means a kind of knowledge: the tree of knowledge of good and evil (see Genesis 2:9b).

There is also the tree of life (see Genesis 2:9b, 3:22b). In Proverbs 3:13, 18, wisdom has been personified as a tree of life; and where there is life, there is automatic death for a curse. Psalms 1:3 talks about the blessed man as a tree by the riverside that bears much fruit and prosperity. And in Revelation 22:2 the tree of life bears twelve manners of fruit and the leaves of the tree are for the healing of the nations.

We cannot as humans do what we have not seen. So humans must see God's Word, run with it, and God will perform what He has said in His Word. Moses had a rod in his hand, but in the spirit, it was an anointed staff and authority to confront governmental powers and bring deliverance to the Jews (see Exodus 4 onward). Every natural thing gives interpretation to spiritual things.

EVERY NATURAL THING
EXPLAINS SPIRITUAL TRUTH

Every physical object exists in nature to explain a spiritual mystery. The spiritual sense of every natural thing is known when the veil is removed. Revelation then is the removal of veils on covered things. Every natural object is operable to correct a spiritual error. We use circumstantial conditions to highlight spiritual life. This is even the reason why Jesus was born during the Roman invasion of the Middle East. Though the promise to bruise the head of the serpent was issued immediately after the fall of man in Genesis 3, it was not until the fullness of time that God sent forth His Son (see Galatians 4:4).

The fullness of time happened in the early period of the reign of the Roman Empire in Israel so that we better understand the kingdom character of God and His destination as God's children. Sometimes Jesus said, "The kingdom of God is like," or "The kingdom of heaven is like" (Mark 4:26 NIV and Matthew 13:31, respectively). And He always used natural things (parables) to explain spiritual things.

The model and system of the Roman Empire gave credence and better explanation of the Kingdom of God; more than any other kingdom that ever existed. Notwithstanding, each and every kingdom contributed to the whole puzzle and helped us all to understand God better. Jesus drew natural and human typological scenes to interpret the Kingdom of God, as we see in all the parables and all His illustrative teachings.

Any time Christ said, "The Kingdom of God [or Heaven] is like," He was using a figurative expression known as a simile to make a comparison and also instruct spiritual truth through a natural pattern. That is, the significance of natural things is to explain spiritual things; and if one wants to understand spiritual things, one must look at how natural examples manifest.

So, for example, the Senate of the Roman Empire was called *Ecclesia,* and He used this terminology to signify the church. Human systems and efforts are all manifestations of spiritual realities. We see through and get revelations for spiritual platitudes and elevations. How deep we can see from the third degree (sight) determines how we will also understand interpretations of spiritual things for our elevation on earth.

EVERY NATURAL THING INTERPRETS A SPIRITUAL MISINTERPRETATION

Romans 1:20 (KJV) states, "For the invisible things of him from the creation of the world are clearly seen, being understood by the things that are made, even his eternal power and Godhead; so that they are without excuse."

We have inherited many misinformations from the day we were born till date. And it has caused the aberrations we possess. Instead of us starting from A to B, we start from A and wander as nomadic rangers, on and on and on to other irrelevant positions, before we come to B.

From our parents and family members, our communities, the schools we attended, and teachers who taught us, our friends in one way or the other may have contributed to the myths and wrong explanations we have to problems. We make assumptions outside facts. We carry facts outside truths, and we know truths but we lack the ability and capacity to master their applications.

The misinformation has given birth to misinterpretations and they have also positioned us in the wrong paradigms causing us to wander about. And we have approached the Bible with these defeats, which affects our thinking and capacity to interpret truths and apply them correctly. Hence, what do we see? We don't even see the way we must. I believe that by now, if the captured principles previously discussed above are rightly considered, then we can move on to the other level where each one of us must endeavor to see something and get something.

Chapter 4

YOU MUST SEE SOMETHING TO GET SOMETHING

I believe we have not forgotten that I have chosen a text as the foundation for this book, the often quoted popular and loaded verse in Proverbs 29:18a (KJV). We must consider its relevance again. It says and I quote, "**Where there is no vision, the people perish.**"

The New International Version defines vision in this verse as a "revelation": "Where there is no **revelation**, people cast off restraint." And the New Living Translation calls vision in this verse "divine guidance": "When people do not accept **divine guidance**, they run wild."

I believe we probably have come across this Scripture in many motivational books and have heard it from Pentecostal/charismatic pulpits several times. Perhaps we have even memorized it right from the beginning of reading this particular book and can quote it offhand many times. Millions of people around the globe have an opinion on this particular verse; however, the problem is in its application.

In fact, it is one powerful biblical instruction; even non-Christians love quoting it because of the practical wisdom it offers. But the reality of life is that if we can't see and imagine, we can't get anything out via sight excursions. If you wish to get something in life, it means you have to master in the primaries the ability to see everything with a positive eye and in an elevated sense of thinking.

If we can see something, we can get something. But when we see nothing, we have sown the seed of nothing into the soil of life and therefore we get nothing. Both poor and rich people are seers and sowers. Poor people see and sow empty things but rich people see and sow substances and faith.

People with nothing are nothing seers and "sowers" and people with something are something seers and "sowers." Every one of us sees and sows and reaps; but what we see and sow determines what we reap. We can only discipline ourselves because of what we have seen and strive hard against all living odds to accomplish them as actualized dreams.

Once we have a dream, we must struggle to realize it and get the dream fulfilled. We must always remember that we see something to get something. If one sees nothing, one gets nothing. The result of what we get or have is the act of what we see. Something occurs for something to happen and nothing occurs for nothing to occur in time. Every one of us is sowing a seed of something or nothing every time of our life. What we sow is what we have seen. What we see is what we will sow. We can be busy sowing and can get engaged and preoccupied in nothing. The interest of the visionary is the thing he has seen; and nothing must interest him except the unique thing he sees and visualizes.

Visionaries always see what others don't see and others don't see what they see. And so he also discusses what others don't discuss and vice versa. This engages conflict between the two groups of people. The most dangerous situation a visionary can ever experience is to grow among people who don't see what he sees. Such people can easily become one's enemy and opposition force. And their opposition can manifest in various forms—hidden and open ones. In this case, many will be jealous and scheme to oppose the vision in diverse ways.

No doubt Jesus had to go through it too. There were a lot of people who plotted against Him in order for Him to fail. There were those enemies who came to His meetings in order to ask Him what they thought were inescapable tricky questions so that they could trap Him down. They called Him names and said He was demon-possessed.

They scorned Him as a carpenter's son and a false prophet from a slum region in Israel. People laughed at Him as a glutton when He ate like humans do. He was even accused of doing things by the devil. Christ's persistence in His vision made Him stand out from all visionaries and we can look at His example and pursue our persuasive vision assignment too.

There is the need for positive people in a visionary's life and no matter how many people may oppose the assignment, some people will emerge whose responsibility will be to protect and defend the vision and the visionary. Jesus upon all that was said about Him had twelve guys around him. Peter cut the ear of Malchus because of his belief in Christ Jesus (see John 18:10). We can see and believe and we can believe and see; all is well when what we see or believe is in line with the principle of purpose and the power of human assignments. We see and create bold visions and influence our world despite what others may think of us.

There is a reason for conflict when some people can't see anything. The world's 7 billion plus people on earth are divided into two categories of nations. Those who see positively and boldly create what they see for the world and those who can't see positively and therefore also create difficulties for the world. But we should be able to influence people and win them over to see what God sees of them. We can do this as visionaries. Oh, yes we can! This way, our vision can be cooperative. A synergic venture of hyper-human initiated effort can take place; and it can win the world. Don't walk alone and sow something relevant, else you die alone on the way.

Walt Disney saw nothing else apart from the cartoons of Disney World. He baited the world to think like him and he created a passion for the cat and mouse cartoon. Every home loves Tom and Jerry. Our world is divided into pro and anti Toms and Jerrys. Who do you always support in this case, Tom or Jerry? But before Disney World was created, Walt Disney got fired and struggled for nearly five years. He lost his job and was accused of lacking imagination; yet, his imagination made him a multi-billionaire before his death. There is no easy road in life. We only have vision roads and pathways. We can also see and die empty in this generation.

Evander Holyfield wasn't stronger than Iron Mike Tyson by natural endowed strengths. But he visualized and saw himself win the bout many times before the fight; he ended up knocking down the undisputed champion and carried the crown away. If God will bless us, He will educate us to visualize and see His blessings, then we can get His blessing. Many people are not blessed in the world because when God is pointing them to the sight of seeing they are waiting in the courtroom of doubt—blind.

We craft and create our own world in this life. It is always a double world in this life. Architects craft their worlds before they create them. Sculptors and artists mold and design their works in their minds' eyes before they create physical objects. We should skillfully design and articulate our world and get out of poverty to prosperity, ill health to good health, foolishness to wisdom, among others. Let's see prosperity and some miraculous hands will pull prosperity to our parlor. As people, we may not be comfortable with this statement. But the truth of it cannot be denied.

Many people are poor because of three major sequential mental visualizations: they see poverty, think poverty, and imagine poverty. They fear to be rich; hence, they get poorer. But God hasn't denied any man prosperity. We deny ourselves prosperity.

If what we see is what we get, then we better decide that we will see what is only good and best in life. If we want to be the best we must see the best. If we want to be wise, we must see wisdom. If we desire to become an uncommon billionaire, we must begin to see billions written to our accounts—billion euro contracts, consignments, associates, and billions everywhere. The first stage of our billion blessings will start when we start to think and live them. What if we want to fly? Then, we must see ourselves as pilots or passengers in an aircraft. What we want to be is what we should be prepared to see. And when we have seen it, let's go and take it from where it is found; we will get it.

One can never go beyond what he sees. And one's speed and distance action will determine and influence his success in this present generation. We should not speed as the wheels and never cover any distance.

We must speed and at the same time cover miles and miles of success. It is not just about our participation; it is about our effectiveness, influence, and efficiency in our participation.

The Concorde flew just like any other jet did. But the influence, efficiency, and effectiveness of the Concorde made it the most influential smart jet ever created and manufactured. It flew at a speed of 1,354 miles per hour (twice the speed of sound). Thus, it flew about twenty-two miles per minute 72,000 feet above sea level. The Mercedes Benz 600, at its ultimate, spins at nine thousand revolutions per second and this gives meaning to the fact that it runs faster, more efficiently, and smoother than any other car. So our outer shape is not necessary here but our in-built structure is.

We can be limited in what we see if we don't equip, fortify, and strengthen our incapacities. We reach what we see and stop there. Everybody in life goes for what he sees and keeps on getting what he sees. When we equip and empower our thinking and thoughts to suit advancement and development we get it. For example, if one's vision or desire is to stay in a skyscraper and there is none in his or her country, what does such an individual do? He can only change his country and go where he finds one; for example, New York. Acts 17:26 (KJV) serves as a key for geographical change: "And [God] hath made of one blood all nations of men for to dwell on all the face of the earth, and hath determined the times before appointed, and the bounds of their habitation." It will be much easier to get a skyscraper in New York City than in one's cottage. Hence, due to what one sees he may also have to do some geographical changes to suit getting what he sees.

One major weakness of the human mind is the defective pathology and the unfortunate belief that some races and cultures are superior to others. When a person feels superior over the other, he stifles and freezes the potential ability of the marginalized, unless he or she is very strong internally to overcome such social vices and negative assumptions against him or her. When it relates to humans, none of us is better than the other. We all are of one blood and one life known as human life. In the psychology of "the power of positive seeing," we must not be influenced by what others necessarily think about us, but we must see ourselves in relationship to our God-given visions and purposes.

We are what God thinks, sees, and says about us and not vice versa. For example, the geographical identity of our orientation isn't the true source of our lives as humans, but our true identity as humans is discovered in God—our source and origin. Where we come from on earth can be assumed to be the touch point by which we land on the earth from Heaven. So we have specific identities and cultures to suit our existence on earth. This shows that we only identify our geographical areas to achieve our God-created visions and assignments on earth.

In other words, whether one is black, white, red, or otherwise, means that one originates from God. No person has proper claims over a particular geographical landscape as his own bonafide property in the eyes of God. For example, no individual from any part of the world be it Ghanaian, American, Indian, Italian, etc., has an absolute claim of dominion over territories.

The ideological school of thought in reference to racism—either in color difference, discrimination, segregation, marginalization, humiliation, deprivation, compartmentalization, or class differentiation—is wrong and has no place in the eyes of God no matter how popular we might have made it. We should endeavor to remain focused in the positive power of our God-given visions and purposes.

Therefore, because of the aforementioned, people are psychologically attuned to the fact that the earth regions we landed on via our biological homes and countries of origin are just touchdown airports to the earth realms. These circumstances have resulted or given rise to the movements of people on earth. There is the assumption that each one of us has rights and is qualified to live anywhere on earth as one wishes without restrictions.

Probably, that is why I am found here in Europe and currently in Copenhagen, Denmark. So, migration and the issues of immigration cannot be eliminated in the world. We, therefore, advise that anywhere one finds his or herself is home and he must learn how to apply his life to the rules and regulations that govern such land to enable him to claim dominion over the land as propagated and assigned by God.

For example, we remember the life of Mother Teresa of Calcutta, India, who understood this spiritual concept of vision assignments and therefore, lived her life to the full in fulfilling it. History has it that she was born Yugoslavian, in Europe (Albanian-Macedonian); but moved to India for her purpose assignment, which truly manifested in her deep sense of passionate vision in the eradication of poverty among the people of India in particular and the world in general. She said, and I quote, "Do not wait for leaders; do it alone, person to person." Mother Teresa didn't wait for anyone before embarking on her vision assignment, one that has helped the entire world irrespective of the fact that she lived in India, far away from her place of origin till death.

General Ojukwu, a one-time Nigerian army general, said to his people, "We should stop the continuous running because of ethnic problems; rather, we should stay fast anywhere we are and be courageous to fight and conquer whatever problem thereof." Of course, he who runs away lives to fight another day. As visionaries, we should move according to purposes and fight the odds, which may militate against our progress.

No matter the type of problems we encounter we can overcome them by our harmonized faith and quality perseverance. When we look at all these circumstances, we can easily agree to the fact that everywhere on earth is fit for the development of our God-given assignments and purposes and therefore no one should be intimidated or victimized in any geographical location.

The Three Areas of Circumstances

Ordinarily, humans are symbolically divided into three major groups in the world:

- People under circumstances

- People who are victims of circumstances

- People who are creators of their own circumstances

The first group of people is composed of those who are pressured in life to toe a certain direction even if it is against their wishes. The second group of people is composed of the victims of circumstances because they are mainly victimized and cannot do anything whatsoever. This group of people is mostly disadvantaged, and no matter what they do they only succumb and cannot overcome their plights.

The third group is composed of creators of their own circumstances and they determine the course of their own life without much external influence. Visionaries operate from the third dimension, where they develop and master the skill of creating circumstance in order not to fall victims to any circumstance and go under a circumstance. And they do this through the positive power of leaning on God to see beyond the human limitations and operate in God's infinite revelations.

THE IMPORTANCE OF "SEEING BEYOND" IN RELATION TO GOD'S VISIT TO ABRAHAM

One day, God visited Abraham in his tent house and said to him, "Do not be afraid, Abram. I am your shield, your exceedingly great reward" (Genesis 15:1b). In verse 2 Abram replied, "Lord GOD, what will You give me, seeing I go childless, and the heir of my house is Eliezer of Damascus?" It was as if Abram was saying, **"How do you become my 'exceeding great reward' when I am childless?"**

Notice the word "seeing" in verse 2. It's a continuous present tense. Abraham by then kept seeing childlessness, so Sarah was still barren. What he saw of Sarah was what he got. Your "seeings" must be in the present continuous positive tenses and not negatives. The fullest conversation is not written in all details. But we can deduce in passing that some events actually occurred during God's visit to the great man of faith.

Abraham had just completed the daily hard work routine and had retired to rest. Remember what we studied previously. We established the principal point that our natural senses should be dead in order to receive spiritual and revelatory experiences. God always speaks but we don't get it well all the time. We often get God's direction and instructions passively as humans. We get them well when we are devoid of our active human senses.

One way we lose our senses is when our natural brain cells are dormant and inactive or while sleeping. When we sleep, the significance is overwhelming. Our natural body recuperates and gets strength. On the other hand, our spirit becomes actively engaged in spiritual communication with God. So God speaks to give us personal instruction through dreams and visions (see Job 33:14-17). Everybody dreams and it means that God speaks to every human being.

In our present dispensation, dreams and visions are multiplied in God's dealings with humans. Joel 2:28 (KJV) confirms the truth: "And it shall come to pass afterward, that I will pour out my spirit upon all flesh; and your sons and your daughters shall prophesy, your old men shall dream dreams, your young men shall see visions." This also means that one must develop the ability to hear from God and obey His instructions.

Where one stands determines and also influences what one sees and even how that individual sees. If we can catch high elevated visions, we must step out from the matchbox houses and come into the open. The vision we apply ourselves to in life is due to where we are standing. And we can apply ourselves to higher and bigger visions when we step out from our own limited geographical positions to God's unlimited geographical points.

GOD INSTRUCTED ABRAHAM TO GET OUT OF THE TENT

Then God spoke to Abraham to get out of his tent into the open space and look up into the skies (see Genesis 15:5). God made Abraham change position. God carried him from a lower dimension to a higher dimension. God repositioned Abraham for a better disposition. God elevated his thinking from the human sense to the elevated divine sense.

The instructions of God through dreams and visions and otherwise, are meant to reposition us to the place God can use us for kingdom assignments and purposes. And our act of obedience will definitely produce God's act of blessing and elevation. This act of obedience helped to engage Abraham's spirit in a symbolic mental manner concerning his future blessings. Why? Because the tent was a limitation to his sight.

Where we choose to stand without the direction of God is always a limitation to our God-intended progress and elevation. I believe Abraham's position at that particular time of the visit was not the right location; and hence, he needed a repositioning for a better disposition.

Seeing all God wanted him to grasp meant he had to have a positive change in direction. He was in the tent and therefore could not see far enough. He came out of the tent and saw all God meant to show him. The secret of successful people is discovered in the strength to obey God's instructions. People who obey God get His blessings and it manifests as success and prosperity.

This indicates that when one is confined in the "tent thinking tradition," he can't see what God wants to show him; and therefore, no matter what, one must come out of the tent. As Abraham obeyed and lifted up his eyes, he saw what God wanted him to see. We also see what God wants us to see if only we will come out from our self-designed positions.

Certainly, it was the constellations of the skies and the galaxies decorated with the stars. Then God spoke into Abraham's heart to give him the vision that his descendants would be like the stars that cannot be counted (see Genesis 15:5). Every natural thing is a symbol God uses to illustrate your elevated personal blessing when you obey the insignificant instruction God gives.

You see, Abraham had some "personal issues." He had no child with Sarah because the womb of Sarah had receded; she was barren. How then was he going to increase and be like the uncountable stars?

Abraham's answer to God reveals some of his personal problems. In life, your answers to questions reveal your weaknesses and strengths, which also often help in getting solutions. Our answers to questions determine what type of help we can get from ourselves. Abraham's answer to God was as if he had said, "How do I become this thing You said, seeing in reality that I have no child?" (see Genesis 15:2-3). God then had to change Abraham's views on how and what he saw and imagined to how God sees and imagines. The dangerous delusion for today's believer is that he might probably never assume the higher thoughts and ways of God. So he never sees the higher things of God. Isaiah 55:7-11 (KJV) speak boldly:

> *Let the wicked forsake his way, and the unrighteous man his thoughts: and let him return unto the LORD, and he will have mercy upon him; and to our God, for he will abundantly pardon. For my thoughts are not your thoughts, neither are your ways my ways, saith the LORD. For as the heavens are higher than the earth, so are my ways higher than your ways, and my thoughts than your thoughts. For as the rain cometh down, and the snow from heaven, and returneth not thither, but watereth the earth, and maketh it bring forth and bud, that it may give seed to the sower, and bread to the eater: So shall my word be that goeth forth out of my mouth: it shall not return unto me void, but it shall accomplish that which I please, and it shall prosper in the thing whereto I sent it.*

Many times, God wants to get closer to us in order for Him to get the opportunity to change our perception and points of view. Abraham discarded his personal views and opinions and immediately assumed a higher dimension and sense of elevation. This profound belief helped to elevate the man's perception in the ability to see things from a positive direction. Finally, Abraham was elevated as the father of faith, the righteous one, a friend of God, and the blessed man.

Normally, there is no human elevation unless there's God's revelation. And there is no God's revelation unless there is God's thought. Therefore, it is of paramount importance that the desire for breakthrough is the strength to break from our own human thoughts and learn how to cruise into God's thought patterns.

And as Abraham believed in God's view, it was also accounted to him for righteousness (see Genesis 15:6). He believed and never staggered from there. He hoped against hope until the dream visualized and a child cried on the lap of Sarah when she was a 90-year-old woman. This picture became the illustrative symbol of Abraham's greatness and enlargement because God made him to see beyond the tent and he was blessed beyond human imagination.

As a matter of fact, the tent also shows the great man's limited sights and imaginations as well as the universal man. If God wants us to get more, He will change our positions and perceptions to see what He has in stock for us. What we see therefore without God does not help us realize our blessings on earth. That is to say, that the similarity of the tent shows our individual little thinking and imagination. So God shifts our minds from our personal positions unto His higher positions to get His blessings as children of Abraham (see Galatians 3:6-9).

In a nutshell, we must know that as believers the ability to see beyond the skies is what we will get if we learn how to position our lives in God. Jesus, the offspring of Abraham, said to His disciples, "The works that I do he [you] will do also; and greater works than these he [you] will do" (John 14:12b). Can you see it?

We should realize that nothing in this world has the power to limit us more than our poor perception and inability to see correctly in God's own direction. We are generally guided by our innate ambitions so that what we often imagine is what we get and not what other people think of us.

Jim Carey, the great Hollywood actor, had nothing but poverty circumstance surrounding him. However, he turned poverty to prosperity because, in his mind, he envisaged prosperity and not poverty. As a persistent person, he was not ready to take no for an answer when it came to his persuasive visions. He had a strong desire to withstand every opposition that came his way.

Once we reject poverty, we can so easily embrace prosperity. Jim changed the way he saw life because he visualized prosperity. Though in reality he had nothing but the empty world of abundance before he pulled some resources together to become a great million-aire, he began to see prosperity and fortune from his inner spirit.

Once the mind conceives something important, it releases something vital for human progress. For example, when the mind conceives good ideas, it helps to release relevant information, which supports the progress of mankind. He once said that he saw himself have a check written in his name into his private account. He woke up and wrote a 10-million-dollar check and placed it in the center of a file.

He looked at it daily until he won the film contract for *The Mask*, which helped him to become a real and an uncommon millionaire. The initial paycheck he received was what he once envisaged, which was 10 million dollars. This logical power of positive seeing reveals the need to realize our dreams. It also helps to show that we must endeavor to claim our possessions from wherever they are in the world.

Oftentimes, some of us don't make it in this world because we lack the sense of sight and imagination. Therefore, it is crucial for us to learn how to fix our minds on what we intend to be and to achieve. That is, as vision-minded people, we should cultivate the rich cultural value system of inscribing the intended success life we desire to cele-brate in the future and learn how to detail every intention on papers; and struggle to accomplish it.

One will collide with destiny and succeed as if some invisible forces pulled resources into the person's garage. The future will reward every effort one makes, and to one's surprise, somebody will help push the person to the future he so desires. What a person sees matters most because it will determine what he will eventually get and become in the future.

In this case, we also must learn how to see rightly. Seeing rightly just means seeing possibilities and not impossibilities. Seeing right ensures that we see faith circumstances and not doubtful circumstances. Seeing right means we must learn how to appreciate and develop the positive power of living a Christ-centered lifestyle. When one is able to see possibilities, faith, and good virtues, one is then ten miles ahead of his peers. You will be surprised to win over challenges and get the right people around you for your dreams and goals to be accomplished faster than you ever thought.

Again, how important will it be for a person who desires vision success to learn how to get the vision accomplished now without procrastinations! An adage says that "procrastination is the thief of time and purposes." Time has never been a friend to anyone on earth except those who can hold it by the tail and use it appropriately to accomplish their purposes. A faith action is an element that holds time in our daily lives and uses it to accomplish our vision purposes on earth. Note that faith in this particular context means the force and action that captivates time, which helps us to realize our dreams on earth.

And, why must a person learn how to develop and master the beautiful art of seeing now? The answers may be attributed to the following reason: our future is designed by what we see. We are encouraged or discouraged by what and how we see. People see us the way we see ourselves. The definition of one's life is based on how one sees oneself.

We reflect in the eyes and minds of people we meet and associate with and they see us based on how we see ourselves. We consciously or unconsciously can become what we see and desire. Our imagination is reflected in the faith of what we see. People respond to us by how they see us and we get the consequences of what we see because what we see determines how we feel. Every future generation (posterity) inherits the legacies of what their forefathers saw.

So as visionaries, I implore that we master the skillful art of the power of positive seeing and change our world once at a time. We can't afford to see anyhow and look anyhow and think that everything is all right with us.

SOMETIMES MINORITY ARE WINNERS; MAJORITY DOES NOT ALWAYS CARRY THE VOTE

Oftentimes, majority opinion does not always carry the vote. However, in democratic setups, the majority carries the vote notwithstanding. In the system or set up of God's Kingdom, the minority can be winners in terms of God's definite intentions and purposes.

In this case, I want to unveil one of the most powerful examples from the Bible that changed my personal life. The books of Numbers (chapters 13-14) and Joshua (chapters 11, 15) elevated my thinking from conforming to public opinions to transforming to kingdom opinions when I saw that Joshua and Caleb stood as a minority group and yet carried the opinion and purposes of God for Israel and defeated the Anakim.

The fact that everybody agrees and accepts an opinion doesn't really mean that the general acceptance makes it correct. For instance, who said, "It can't be done"? It can be done if one applies himself to it and time will tell. Who says, "This dream isn't impossible"? All things are possible to him that believes (see Mark 9:23). Who says, "One has failed"? You only fail if you refuse to try again. But once you keep on trying nobody can label you as a failure.

The moment of failure is the consequence of thinking that one cannot endeavor again. So you see, one must condition the mind to seek the opinion of God and act on it more than what he believes out of what people say. The two young men, Joshua and Caleb, therefore inspire me to take concrete decisions always based on God's opinion and not circumstances or peoples' opinion about a circumstance.

Moses sent spies for espionage activity in the land of the Canaanites. He instructed them, "Go up this way into the South, and go up to the mountains, and see what the land is like" (Numbers 13:17b-18a). We see the response of the spies in verses 26-33:

Now they departed and came back…Then they told him, and said: "We went to the land where you sent us. It truly flows with milk and honey, and this is its fruit. Nevertheless the people who dwell in the land are strong [stronger than us] … we saw the descendants of Anak [giants who are over ten feet tall] there…the people whom we saw in it are men of great stature. There we saw the giants (the descendants of Anak came from the giants); and we were like grasshoppers in our own sight, and so we were in their sight."

Note here that the giants didn't see them as grasshoppers. They saw themselves as such, so whatever they heard seemed grasshopper mentality to them. In a real-life situation, it is not what one sees that matters most; it is how one sees that matters the most. As believers, we should not conform to our negative circumstances and confess them as they are. We must learn how to conform to the Word of God and confess the life-transforming Word upon our negative circumstances.

Actually, the giants saw them but their consideration of who they were was designed by how they saw themselves. Joshua and Caleb were the minority opinion and they saw differently from the majority and they changed the wrong perception of the people to the way God thought of the people in the land. A person must always see differently to think differently.

Often, we see, think, and imagine by our own circumstance. But if we walk with God, then we must cultivate and nurture His thoughts and His ways to get things according to His plans. This will elevate our human circumstance to a higher degree of spiritual excellence and erect God's circumstance over the prevalent situation.

LET'S REPLACE HUMAN SYSTEMS WITH KINGDOM MODELS

As a child of God, I have been taught to be very careful regarding how, where, and what I can possess. But I feel it is the system of this world that limits kingdom views on achievements; and therefore

I must replace these erroneous systems with the kingdom models. The kingdom model teaches that anywhere the soles of our feet step on, our God has given it to us as an inheritance. This means that almost everything one desires and where he desires it, he must have it in life.

Therefore, all one must do is to create the necessary channels that will generate a lot of fortunes that will help him realize his dreams. If one sees himself possessing lands and properties, one will get them no matter where he is living. We must buy lands and properties for our future as kingdom citizens. If we see it here, we can also get it here, and if we see it there, we can get it there. Therefore, I believe it is of rich blessings to see them here and there so that one will begin to travel on demand according to purpose assignment on earth.

THE EDIT (LAW) OF GOD FOR KINGDOM PEOPLE

As believers we should consider the fact that the Kingdom of God has a model, which we must understand. The kingdom model is the law of God, which we must always obey. These laws can be summed up as the laws of obedience and success. When we comply with the rules and laws of God, He in turn rewards us with blessings, no matter where we may be. One such law of obedience and success is written as an edict of God to us in the book of Jeremiah.

Let's read Jeremiah 29:4-7 (KJV):

Thus saith the LORD of hosts, the God of Israel, unto all that are carried away captives, whom I have caused to be carried away from Jerusalem unto Babylon; Build ye houses, and dwell in them; and plant gardens, and eat the fruit of them; Take ye wives, and beget sons and daughters; and take wives for your sons, and give your daughters to husbands, that they may bear sons and daughters; that ye may be increased there, and not diminished. And seek the peace of the city whither I have caused

*you to be carried away captives, and pray unto the LORD for it:
for in the peace thereof shall ye have peace.*

Therefore, if one finds himself outside of his place of origin, one must still live and organize his life in the place in order to be successful. We must not forget the race and geographical issues we raised in the previous chapters, which help us to know that we belong to the whole earth and not only a part of the earth. That is to say, we are walking in disobedience when we live in places as foreigners and hence, do not contribute our quota to the development of the region. In this particular teaching, we understand that God commanded us to build houses, marry wives, and give our children for marriages and procreate abundantly until we occupy the place. As we engage in the development of where we are, so shall we equally be developing in our personal lives.

➤ Catch a Vision and Conquer the World

Never forget that we are still discussing the issue of cultivating the strength to see rightly in our world and conquer our world through the positive power of seeing. And we must once again quote the rich wisdom nuggets King Solomon offered us in his generation. Where there is no vision the people cast off restraint and go on rioting or rampages (see Proverbs 29:18a). One may ask why we have to quote it again. It's okay to ask. But like I said right from the beginning, we will quote it several times. When a person hears a particular statement repeatedly, he soon becomes so familiar with it and the statement somewhat impacts with mesmerizing effect so that the reader can understand the importance. Well, that is the very reason I have made "the spirit of seeing and imagining" the theme of this book. I have come a long way to accept the axiom that **repetition is the mother of invention** and what you see is what you will be getting soon in the distant future.

Nothing comes to us but what we see ourselves imagine in history. Do not foozle this reality because everybody sees. But some people see nothing out of something and therefore hardly fancy and admire anything. And some see something out of nothing and therefore cherish and celebrate. Such great gifted minded people will always see something and get something important out of it. This group of people can be termed the wise and great people who discern, recognize, and celebrate the future successes in whatever they see and appreciate.

The Positive Power of Repetition Can Make Us See What We Desire

This issue of repetition can be related to Sir Thomas A. Edison for his reputed experiments on the electric bulb invention—repeated for a record 1,000 times. Can one imagine how boring it could be that the same experiment was repeated for one thousand times? And yet he still had the courage to continue until he succeeded. And Thomas Edison reportedly locked himself up for eight to nine days in his laboratory working on the experiments. So this man didn't just get a breakthrough for the electric bulb. It came by perspiration and not just inspiration.

Inspiration is the passionate and strong desire to achieve something. But perspiration is the energy required to achieve something. He applied himself to hard work through his dream and vision and produced light. Thomas Edison could do all this due to his effort on strong vision—to give the world electric light, which has paid off and all of us are beneficiaries now. Never forget that God is a dreamer and he loves people who dream. He gives visions and dreams and He loves people who love to dream big and He makes them great on earth.

Hence, one should not be tired of learning all one can do and even reading as many books as possible until one succeeds. A person should endeavor to develop himself to the highest level in order to achieve success and not just money. We must realize that money is the inferior reason why people work. People should work because of their purposes and not because of money. Everybody must learn how to hang on for a while in every difficult step he takes when he is convinced about the purpose of the work. We must try to endure what pressurizes us and break our necks till we succeed. Perseverance and persistence with the spirit of consistency will break the strength of every opposition in our lives. The fact that you are reading this book suggests to me that you are also a vision addict and I believe you will equally succeed in life just as Thomas Edison and others have done.

Everything Once Existed as a Mere Idea

The fact is that everything once existed in nature as a mere idea, whether tangible or intangible. One can look at any of the giant corporations and will realize that they all started as mere ideas in a person's mind. It's obvious that people with great ideas rule this world. Every single issue once existed in God's mind as a mere dream. And as humans, every single issue equally exists as mere dreams and we can transmute every single idea to something significant if we apply time and strength to our efforts. It's also reported that over forty thousand ideas invade and run through the minds of all humans in a day. But some people are more willing to catch on those ideas and use them to make an impact in the world.

God first forms great ideas in His mind and secondly creates them from His mind. It's paramount to know that there is always a first mental creation before there is a second physical creation. Long before the Creator passionately declared, "Let there be light....Let us make man in our image, after our likeness" (Genesis 1:3a, 26a KJV), those creative words were in His mind and those were His dreams and visions, which came out as creative stories and narratives in the Bible.

As we are also created in the image and likeness of God, we likewise form great ideas in our own minds and create them into our world. Everything we see was once an idea. And ideas, as rich as they are, come to all men of all races, cultures, and religions, but some people are smarter and more willing to initiate these ideas into positive results than others. Normally, we can deduce from the above discussion that the first car was first visualized and imagined in the minds of the manufacturer before it was driven on the road. The Wright brothers conceived the first plane before it was manufactured and seen in the airports. Therefore, if one can ever create something right now, he must first build the idea of the thing in the mind before he can invent it.

Let's remember that the inventions and manufacturing of things always begin as ideas in the minds before they are realized.

It does not matter how the word *vision* has been used, its relevance and vitality makes it stand the test of time. As a matter of fact, vision is a principle and principles are permanent and unalterable. Dr. Stephen R. Covey, the author of *First Things First* (Free Press, 1994) and *The 7 Habits of Highly Effective People* (Free Press, 2003), believes that "all the wishing and even all the work in the world if it's not based on valid principles, will not produce quality-of-life results. It's not enough to dream. It's not enough to try. It's not enough to set goals or climb ladders. It's not enough to value. The effort has to be based on practical realities that produce the result." Visionaries will live and die; yet their visions and principles—if they don't have permanent value to live on—will be forgotten. Any vision that dies before the demise of the visionary is not a true principle and vision.

There Is Coordination between People and Vision

WHERE THERE IS NO VISION PEOPLE PERISH, AND WHERE THERE IS NO PEOPLE VISION PERISHES OR NEVER EXISTS. Let us pause for a moment and reflect on this powerful statement above. What comes to one's mind when a visionary joins together with others as a coordinating team for the accomplishment of a dream? They can go into a state of joy and melancholy because a definite idea is caught, and they will equally enjoy the benefits of a specific goal.

One then will see how the people have responded to their visions and ideas. For every vision to achieve results, the visionary must coordinate efforts with people. Every visionary must be able to recognize other people's influence on his vision and connect strongly to them. And once he can recognize them, some people will automatically be connected in his life. You need to know that one needs to pull out or away from the influences of those he loves if he is going to step respectfully into his God-given vision assignments.

The danger of family or blood ties may be one good reason why God probably tells most of His servants to relocate for the fulfillment of their vision assignments. Every vision has some attraction and distraction and we must recognize this immediately. We need to declare independence from the negative influence of people and get connected and interdependent on positive people when we are on assignment through our missions and visions. I have never been afraid to disassociate myself from potential dream-killers and their subtle religious deceits. I have disassociated myself without confrontation many times because of their pollutions and contaminations.

And equally, I have pushed hard to get connected to some important people who mattered in my career and worked hard to protect such relationships. I have even gone to the extent of sowing seeds of money into some people's lives to receive in return mentorship association. Never ever sow a seed of any kind without expectation of its harvest. Sow and expect!

Visionaries should disassociate themselves immediately from people who are going nowhere and have nothing significant to contribute. And as we get to the right companies and associations, we trigger into operation the principle of synergy. Can one then imagine life without a visionary, or for that matter, people existing without a visionary among them? The life wire of any family, corporation, nation, or group of people is found and centered on their visionary abilities in connecting to those who matter most in their career pursuits.

Oftentimes, a visionary gives vision instructions and a coordinating team member applies the instruction for success. A word from the visionary can move people into unimaginable heights or even set them off like Concorde jets. Such instructions can help the people throughout their lifetimes and ease hard times to eradicate poverty in their world. Such people may end up as world changers and contribute significantly to society. They can do things only God can imagine because they have the opportunity to have a visionary in their lives.

Visionaries have a great ability to influence people around them with a sense of positive sights and visions. They always have the skill and grace to help others to realize their true potentials and energy toward work. The human potential should be released only through the activity of one's work purpose and not job motives.

So, if we release our potential for a job purpose, we abuse our potentials and ourselves altogether. It's vital then for my reader to know what a job is and what one's work is. A job is anything one does on earth to make ends meet; anything you probably do to make money to take care of yourself and the family is a job. Work is different from a job.

One's ability to discover his assigned purpose ushers him to work: the recognition to harmonize a celebration and consolidate in a particular act of performing the assignment God ordained and designed an individual for even before his creation. Nowhere in the Bible does God endorse a job. He always endorses work. We are mandated to work on earth and not to do a job on earth. "Prepare thy work without, and make it fit for thyself in the field; and afterwards build thine house," advised King Solomon in Proverbs 24:27 (KJV).

Nobody can become an uncommon billionaire by doing a job. Matthew Ashimolowo, the pastor of the largest western European church, says that a job is the acronym for "**J**ust **O**ver **B**roke." Work pushes human efforts to the compartment regions of success and wealth. Everybody in the world today who is a billionaire and highly successful is in the work region and not the job region.

As humans, it is clear that our potential lies dormant and latent when we don't have a sense of direction to the particular work God designed for us. Our potentials, because of a lack in vision, can then remain as untapped energy until a visionary fuses them with zeal, passion, and action. The visionary's zeal in influencing people can move them from latent visionaries to active visionaries and bring them the progress that makes required riches and wealth possible. This is the purpose of this book, to help millions of people to identify their designated work, purpose assignments, and vision orientation so that they become skillful and effective citizens of the world.

When an individual is well groomed in vision concepts, that person can easily move his personal vision to action. Corporate vision doesn't mean people have no vision themselves. It means that we must learn how to function in our personal visions in line with the concept the corporate vision postulates and propagates. We agree and align ourselves to the holistic venture of the upper vision and our vision gets fulfilled too.

Hence, one must endeavor to know how to point people to the paradise in the imagination and see them as qualified instruments that help them to realize the vision in their hearts without encroaching on the rights and liberties of others. It's always possible that one's vision can work in another vision for success to be achieved.

Humans, in reality, may not probably need an intellectual orientation in a school before they can participate in vision outputs. Everybody can participate in a vision when he or she gets an orientation about the vision. For example, one doesn't need a scholastic degree in Aristotelian logic, or Herbert Spencer's philosophies, or Albert Einstein's calculus before one can participate in a vision.

What qualifies a person's participation in the development of a vision is his readiness and willingness of mind. Every capable mind must hold on to the fort and supply of his or her mental strength; and together, we can accomplish an unimaginable assignment for the development of humanity.

For example, Martin Luther King Jr. saw the human races as equal and pointed the world in that direction when African Americans were highly discriminated and considered as sub-humans. His actions helped to bring civil rights freedom to African Americans and also helped shape the future of our world and how we think about people of color.

One cannot say that the world is without racism, but the magnitude of racism is reduced drastically due to King's hearty revolution in the 1960s. Richard Dublin, when interviewed in the 2007 issue of Ebony Magazine (Number 11), had this to say, "The difficulty here is parsing out what has to do with color and what has to do with the business. Things have changed that much in that we live in a substantially segregated society, and that's reflected in our media." Harold Perrineau, a film and TV star in Hollywood once said, "What really confuses me more is that as we evolve, people like to be safe in thinking…Black people can only be a certain way. I keep hoping that at some point, things will change." And the truth is that things have changed.

Barack Obama is gone into the Guinness World Records as the first ever African American to have won the presidency on the ticket of the Democrats for black Americans in the history of the United States of America.

Today, Barack Obama and other African Americans have likewise risen to the top of different career heights in the history of the United States of America, which wasn't the case in the past. Wow! Who ever thought of this? That one day an African American would contest for the number one spot in the politics of the United States of America. Humanity has impeded the progress of humanity by criminal acts against one another. Yet, here we are and blacks are occupying many sensitive spots in world affairs.

This reveals that when the human mind is put in a conducive atmosphere, growth is inevitable because it will yield and respond to the four laws of productivity and finally, unto the ultimate reason for human creation—dominion.

It is generally accepted that people don't perish because of the color of their skin, people do not perish because they were unfortunate to acquire higher education in life, and people don't perish because they are victims of a feat or are accursed. The reason why most people perish is because some decide to perish and therefore attract destruction. Some people hide behind the blame game of self-pity and justify their destruction. Often, we see people blame people, circumstances, and things as impediments to their development.

However, the fact is that responsibility is the key of God for success and irresponsibility is the devil's key for destruction. The Bible's language for responsibility and irresponsibility is hard work and laziness, respectively. Hence, I urge my readers to be absolutely resolute and responsible in life and blame no one and nothing as external powers that help ruin one on earth.

This is the secret Oprah Winfrey had as a growing child in a poor American neighborhood. She took responsibility and faced life's challenges by her right attitudes. She developed a strong understanding and belief about herself and what she could do, so she has successfully climbed the ladder of wealth and fame.

She has made it to the top and has attracted the admiration of people. The sweetest part of the story is that everybody can be an Oprah Winfrey if only everybody will learn how to practice her daily routine. We can all become somebody from the position of nobodies. We can evacuate ourselves from the ruins of poverty, negative paradigms, and mundane lifestyles. We can climb to the top and be very successful if only we see it so.

That is also to say that people do perish because they lack the protective perception of a disciplined lifestyle. Some people hardly set standards and rules for themselves, so that they live without any sort of regulation and self-imposed laws. Many people today lack the right life-sustaining fervor called discipline or vision.

Though every one of us has a vision, not all of the visions we have are rightly focused on the perfect will of God. Some visions fall within the context of the passive will of God and men struggle. And some fall outside God's will, so they become evil and human; such visions God opposes vehemently. What this book is trying to do is to position our minds on God-centered visions and also teach us how to remain in God's operative paradigms.

Visionaries Hardly Die

A MAN OF VISION FEARS NO ENEMY AND BELIEVES THAT HE CANNOT DIE WITH HIS GOD-GIVEN VISION. A man of vision sees beyond what fear projects and when he is even surrounded by a vast and intimidating army, he can boldly say, "**Those who are with us, are more than those against us.**" There is always a good reason for walking in the spirit as visionaries. We receive physical manifestation of the things we see in the spirit.

Vision Protects Lives as Can Be Seen in Nelson Mandela

You see, vision protects and preserves life. It was vision that sent Nelson Mandela to prison, and it was vision that kept him alive for those tortuous 27 years. Eventually, it was vision that set him free from the prison, and it was vision that put him on the throne as the first ever black president in post-apartheid South Africa. Vision! I love the sound of that living word—vision. If only we can be self-disciplined and be focused on realizing what we see (of the future), vision will keep us from going wayward. Our best security officer in life is our vision.

THE PERSONAL KEY IS DISCIPLINE

Yes, self-restraint is self-control, self-control is self-discipline, and self-discipline is self-limitation; vision is the salt that seasons visionaries into action and inaction to have a regulatory lifestyle of "dos and don'ts."

IN THIS WAY, WHERE THERE IS NO VISION PEOPLE CAST OFF RESTRAINT. THEY GROW WILD LIKE THE BEAST OF THE FIELDS. We must remember that the difference between mammals and humankind is the spirit and likeness of God in us. When that composition is extracted, we are like animals. And no man can truly see in the perceptive of purpose when he has fallen from this state and composition. And if one is as equal to a beast, then one will live like a beast and cannot be disciplined in any way.

~

"Sub-humanness is not established on racial colors but on our obedience or disobedience on the intents and purposes of God for humans."

—*A. O. Amoabeng*

~

Animals are not disciplined in many senses because they don't have the genes of discipline in them as humans. The fallen human then comes to the same level of a mammal and this is the reason behind human indiscipline. So, humanity and sub-humanity are not established on racial colors but on obedience and disobedience of the intent and purposes of God.

A visionless person cannot live a disciplined lifestyle because he has fallen into absolute disobedience of his intended dominion life. Before salvation, fallen humans are framed with human bodies, but in essence, they are as beasts without a regulated spirit because their human spirit, presented as an image and likeness, is not joined to the Spirit of God. King Solomon wrote that a person without rule over his spirit is like a city without walls (see Proverbs 25:28). In other words, they have no restricted, regulated patterns ingrained in them to function as kingdom representatives on earth.

Their culture and lifestyle are jeopardized and cursed. They are seen everywhere and they say and do everything and have no sense of discipline. Therefore, they have no true dominion breakthroughs. They have sights but they lack insight and they have eyes but they lack the vision required for earth success. Note that even machines function with breaks, how much more humans? The biggest insanity syndrome of the sane is to learn and master the skill to tame and coach mammals when our own tongue is destroying us.

Indiscipline is inevitable without a revolutionary sense of vision spirit, spirit of purpose, focus attitudes, and discernments. A person with vision is restrained and disciplined. Solomon says a person without self-control or self-restraint is like a city: like "China without the great wall of China." The opposite can be applied effectively. Temptations do not lure men. But yielding to temptation destroys. If one is tempted, it doesn't mean one is fallen. Jesus was tempted, yet He never fell (see Matthew 4:1-11). Not every door is an open door to a person or people of vision. Visionaries go only to where their vision directs them, and if the spotted position is dangerous and unrewarding, they restrain themselves. Vision is the nerve center and the live wire of a people who position themselves to see afar in pursuit of purpose.

VISION REQUIRES DISCIPLINE AND FOCUS

A true visionary creates self-imposed rules and regulations. He is no longer "his own man"; he is now controlled by a master-called vision. And because he wants to apply himself to time for skill and expansion, he is going to stay indoors and work himself out on practice, instead of going out with his colleagues to have fun. Personally, my life is wired around my office. I spend most of the hours in the studio applying myself to the nuggets and skill of my calling. It takes discipline to do so because the world's circumstances and issues will attack us in order to share the time allotted.

But discipline becomes the key for perseverance, resistance, persistence, consistence, and constancy. Discipline may mean reading two or more books every month to sharpen your knowledge as a public figure. It's important to listen to great people ahead and apply knowledge the way they think and act to get similar consequences. Let's train ourselves in ceaseless hours as men and women; and we must be careful to avoid distractions such as girls, gold, and glory, or otherwise, women, wealth, and world.

Adversity and unpleasant circumstances mean little to a man of vision. I have had my fair share as a youth and as a man. In fact, all the men and women whose names are found in the faith hall of fame in Hebrews 11 in the Bible are people of vision. They dared to do mighty works and blazed the trail because they were fueled by the exuberant energy of what they saw. When you apply yourself to discipline, you will not dare to be afraid but attempt to achieve your objectives.

A PURPOSE-DRIVEN VISION EMPOWERS AND ACCELERATES SUCCESS

WHEN YOUR VISION IS PURPOSE-DRIVEN, POWER FROM ON HIGH COMES TO FUEL AND ACCELERATE YOUR EFFORTS TOWARD SUCCESS. Vision is the generator of victory in all human endeavors. No matter how long it takes, if you have persisted enough and suffered long on the path of vision-fulfillment, your vision will speak and your success will be achieved. Ultimately, our success or failure in life is determined by our own faith in God as well as our obedience to what He tells us individually.

Visionaries are purpose-driven and not problem-driven. They are answers-givers and solution-makers. We lead a purpose-driven life to be successful and not a problem-driven one to complicate issues in life. Humans as individuals share common traits of problems and one cannot separate himself or herself as problem free. We all apply ourselves to challenges in our live's and seek knowledge to get answers for them. We are constantly confronted by problems or we surmount a problem. The negotiations we make as principles help us use the same problems to get solutions and emerge eventually as champions. Purpose-driven people are empowered and they can accelerate speedily and achieve positive consequences.

THE NAME ABRAHAM ALWAYS CARRIES A BIG TEST BUT ALWAYS SHARES A BIG TESTIMONY

IT TOOK FATHER ABE 25 YEARS OF WAITING, BUT AT THE END, HIS OBEDIENCE TO GOD PAID OFF. Isaac was born and the rest is history. You have heard about another Abe, this time not in the Bible. I am referring to the historic modern-day Abraham Lincoln—former American president. He had one of the most outstanding "biographies of a failure."

His experiences in his time teach us good lessons; they teach us that tough times never last more as tough men do. One can fail, but one isn't a failure. We can fail and we have all failed before, but none of us can be labeled as failures once we keep trying to overcome our circumstances.

In this regard, we then know that as humans we are imperfect and cannot avoid failing sometimes. They are unpreventable but we can use our failures to master great knowledge and discover for ourselves ways through which some things can be achieved. Failure isn't the end result of any circumstance, but the means and processes to the end of it. In this case, we often seem weak and so easily give up. But the reality unfolds and the visionary through the spectacle of positive seeing comes to realize that it's not over until all is over.

As people of purpose and power, we must apply the knowledge of waiting in order to take dominion. It doesn't matter what happens but it matters how one can use what happens to change direction for a positive influence on society. One should consider the rich biography with the failing circumstances of the ex-president of the United States of America and learn from his story.

1. Survived a difficult childhood

2. Had about one year of formal education

3. Failed in business

4. Defeated for the legislature

5. Failed again in business

6. Elected to the legislature the next time he tried

7. Fiancée died

8. Defeated for Speaker

9. Only one of four sons lived past age 18

10. Defeated for Congress but elected for the same position three years later

11. Defeated again for Congress two years later

12. Kept his hope alive because his vision was clearly for the NUMBER ONE spot of the great nation

13. Tried for Vice President and was defeated

14. Tried to enter the Senate two years later but failed

After several decades of pursuing his vision of leading his people, Uncle Abe won the NUMBER ONE SPOT. In the year 1861, ABRAHAM LINCOLN became the president of the United States of America. For the rest of his story, check history and ask the average American.

If it were you, wouldn't you have given up? The sober truth is that often when failure and defeat seem to have become synonymous to our name, we should open our eyes and see afar, for our dreams are about to come true. It is upon some of these powerful historical exposures, among other personal experiences, that I became motivated to write the book entitled, *How Far Can You See?* I am encouraging you to get a hold of that book too and entrench yourself in the powerful virtues of vision concepts and philosophies. That is for our example and encouragement. The vision will speak for you and ultimately position you at a place where your purpose can get fulfilled, so never give up on your dream. Keep on working hard at realizing it. It will come to pass though it tarries.

Chapter 5

OVERCOME EVERY OBSTACLE AGAINST WHAT YOU SEE

It is not what came against us, or the poverty we face. It is how we responded and reacted against what came against us and the poverty that came against us. Henry Stanley Haskins believed that "what lies behind us and what lies before us are tiny matters compared to what lies within us" (as quoted by Stephen R. Covey in his book *The Seven Habits of Highly Effective People*, Free Press, 2003.)

What comes against us externally cannot match up with the power and strength that comes from within us against the very challenge. We succumb or overcome by the right or wrong attitudes against obstacles. Obstacles are everywhere and the ignition fueled in our hearts and minds is powerful and stronger than any dark acts of wickedness in the universe.

A story was once told of a man who the gods predicted would die by a falling tree. So this man avoided the presence of trees. He cut all the trees in his backyard and never visited any park. Unfortunately, as an African who believed in traditions and cultural practices, he bought a local chewing stick and put it on top of a window.

The following morning he tried to pick the stick and it resulted in an accident. He died by the slight hurt from the chewing stick. This lesson teaches us that it's very difficult for man to separate himself from obstacles. We live with them and how we negotiate and overcome or succumb, shows how different we are—strong or weak.

One must desire effective living and not busy lifestyles. How we negotiate the twist and turns in life will determine how effective or ineffective we become. And the fact that we must be effective doesn't also guarantee we become perfectionists. We can be perfect and excellent and not perfectionists. It's known that perfectionists never get satisfied with an excellent result in life and this in itself is a deficiency and an obstacle. A perfect oriented thinker believes in excellence and continuous improvement as a way of going forward in life. We can be effective and articulate and never be perfectionists.

In any way, we can be efficiently effective and still go busy and achieve maximum outputs. But maximum results never come by mere butter cuts; they come by diligence and overcoming harsh odds. Our lives' purposes and visions will face insurmountable difficulties and we can't avoid but face them strongly. We must face and win every difficult circumstance, no matter how long it will take. The success of any vision is the visionary's ability to foresee difficulties ahead and create or establish continuous summations of solutions way back before they emerge. Visionaries formulate summations of dynamic solutions way back before they arise. And the quicker our organization, the quicker the revolution we spin over our difficulties.

You see, a person cannot ever choose what comes at him, but he can choose how to respond to what comes at him. The only thing we can always control is our own attitude in life. We choose everything that happens to us. We decide what we want and don't want; where to go and not to go. Every decision in life is self-made. The bout against circumstance is well developed with our own rich attitudes. Circumstance is never strong until we decide by our own free will to make it strong. Life will not give us what we desire of it unless we make conscientious efforts to fight. One mustn't forget that life is a battle (see 2 Corinthians 10:3-6).

John the Baptist came in the spirit and power of Elijah at the beginning of the New Testament (see Luke 1:17a). From the time of John the Baptist until now (thus, from the end of the law and the prophets to the preaching of the Kingdom of God), the Kingdom of Heaven suffers (permits and allows) violence, but some men of violence snatch and take it with force (see Matthew 11:12-13). We must be aggressive and wild to face life's challenges. It is difficult but it is not above our imagination. It is only difficult when we decide it is so.

Any moment we get the "know-how," it becomes very simple and easy. We are confronted daily by challenges and how we cultivate attitudinal shock absorbers, tells how prepared we were before we began the journey of success. Every obstacle against a person is not strong enough to destroy the person. It means that the person was ill-prepared and if the same person will get prepared the obstacle will melt before him like butter on heat. Proper preparation overcomes difficulties, no matter how they are.

Again, never think that everybody understands one's position as a person. In actual sense, most people misunderstand visionaries when they announce their dreams. It's normal to be misunderstood, but it's abnormal for a visionary to be impeded and blocked to go wayward because he was misunderstood. I want to fight and feel the smell of victory, so I stay on course amidst difficulties and desperations. One painful aspect of vision life is the unlikeliest ability to separate from people because of one's vision. And one dangerous aspect of vision enhancement is growing in the shadow of doubters.

Many visionaries didn't survive because of the presence of predators. Locating the predator and preventing his schemes against the dream is a sure way to win in the vision contest. If we can eliminate the eliminator and terminate the terminator, or destroy the destroyer, the way is cleared and the obstacle is removed. And we cannot wait until all the people agree or endorse our vision dreams and plans before we proceed. In the case of visions and visionaries, some people are always for us and others are always against us. And mainly it's not we the visionaries per se, but the vision we carry.

Herein, as vision carriers we must condition our minds knowing that some people are for us and some are against us, yet life must go on. Some friends will despise and flee our company; new friends will come and join our company, yet life must go on. Some sets of circumstances are for us and others are against us, yet life must go on. Some things are also for us, and some things are against us and yet life must go on.

We have to develop our minds and be wise to choose those things that are for us and avoid all efforts to tame those contradictory things, which are against us. Many people don't care at all about you until perhaps you hit the world news and then they will chase you out of your charms and successes. But when you announce what you see, between your outdoor ceremonies and in the process of accomplishing your intention, there are obstacles to the place of achieving your goals. Obstacles are hidden bridges to the land of blessing. They come via people, set of circumstances, and some other things.

An obstacle can be termed as a resistance force against what one sees and what one must get in definite times. But the good news is that one needs obstacles to push up the adrenaline for speed unto success. You need obstacles in order to be dependent on God and not just your human connectivity and capacities. If for instance, one came in the open and was directly confronted by a hungry and angry lion, does he know he has to run at a speed that will make him a super sprinter? The person may clock an unbeatable time record better than Ben Johnson's, Carl Lewis's, and Morris Green's put together. And the person may not be able to do the same time ever again in his life. The passion and desire to be alive can produce a great measure of inner strength and adrenaline and we can run as never before. Relatively, one shouldn't wait for a lion to chase him before he does the unbeatable. He must do it right now in his mandated assignment.

One major obstacle we must be very conscious of is the obstacle of public opinion. I have addressed part of these issues in the previous chapters and here again because it's crucial to vision success. The pains inflicted by people's opinion about you and your deeds are nonessential for God to respond to your capacity of pursuits either in a dream, goal, purpose, or vision. Visionaries who seek the burden of men more than God fail along the way and their proof of pain is their response. The proof of failure is the adherence to public voices. Voices, which do not promote the welfare of God's will, intent, and purpose, amount to failure and shame. Public opinion can change one's direction and bring him to shame and disobedience as it was in the case of Aaron, the high priest, and Saul, the first king of Israel.

Through the effect of public language concerning who and what we are, as well as what we are assigned to do, we can so easily move our focus and detour in kingdom assignment unto human assignments; what an obstacle! In this case, I urge everyone to master the effective and positive key of controlling public opinion and cross-check every suggestion with the living instruction of God's will, intention, and purpose. This is the only reason that brought Jesus to the cross of Calvary and introduced Him into the Heavens as the King of kings and Lord of lords. And this is one reason a visionary can assume heights and power in his vision glory.

➤ No Man Has the Power to Judge Your Vision Except God

NORMALLY, WHEN A PERSON ANNOUNCES HIS VISION, SOME PEOPLE MAY MOCK HIM, AND MOCKING OR SCORNING IS A GREAT OBSTACLE AGAINST VISION PROGRESS. Some others may wish well, even though they may "realistically" reserve their comments. Others will openly oppose and hate you for what you stand for.

Mostly, those people are devilish, fools, and jealous because they don't know God and they don't understand the definitions of their own individual lives. When a person is in a state of melancholy, he can confuse and obstruct the sane into getting confused and melancholic. But the truth of the matter is that no man has the power to judge your vision except God because He knows the intent, will, and purpose of your life.

External Obstacles versus Our Internal Convictions

Much as we have external obstacles, none is as strong as our internal convictions. As purposed visionaries, we are as strong as a lion to defeat every external obstacle erected against our progress. The dangers to our growth and development are the internal fears we have, and these are our greatest obstacles. It is not what you see, but how you see it.

And it is not just going for what you see, but whether the opposition within you can conquer ahead through the inner conviction. And it is not really the oppositions, but how you negotiate yourself on the way by the right principles and habit ethics. Every person can win over his or her obstacles when he or she keys in the right attitudes within. For attitude is everything in this world and it crashes down any external opposition and difficulty.

The Tobiah and Sanballat Obstacles

When King Artaxerxes rejoiced and supported the vision of reconstructing the broken wall of Jerusalem by Nehemiah, Tobiah and Sanballat heard about the news: "[And] they were deeply disturbed that a man had come to seek the well-being of the children of Israel" (Nehemiah 2:10b).

The spirit of Tobiah and Sanballat is the spirit of the prophets of doom which states, "We will be patient enough to wait for his failure, in order to declare as usual, 'We told you so!'" For such ones, even if one begins to chalk successes, they will still express doubt and try to influence us to "reason up." And if you believe you are too old or less gifted as an individual, you have believed a big lie of the prophet of doom. Who told you this lie you believed? God or those "dammed and doomed"?

The Trinity Bookshop Was a Vision of Mike and Evelyn

What a person sees as a burden is nothing to his neighbor. People don't see and operate from the same spectacles, neither do the neighbors around us. In this case, let's consider the vision a couple had for their city. Mike and Evelyn had a vision in which Christians in Brescia City, Italy, would apply themselves to gaining knowledge in God's Word and purposes.

They believed each human being came to the earth with specific gifts and talents relevant for their leadership success. But the medium through which an individual passes determines how his gift and talent will benefit humanity. They also knew that development or empowerment is the key to gift and talent enhancement. But how they were going to help their city folks was a big challenge.

Will they start a church and teach? Or should they commit themselves to create a friendly resource center for people—a bookshop? They felt a strong need to start a Christian bookshop ministry so that evangelical teachings would become an integral part of the fabric of Italian life.

We must first understand the situation in Italy. In terms of propagation of Pentecostal, charismatic, and evangelical gospel setups, one of the dry places on earth is Italy. The Catholic Church is dominant in Italy and Brescia is not exempted. The city is also a dry place with regard to reading habits of the Africans, even among their leadership.

Generally, Africans in this part of the world hardly read due to the circumstances they find themselves in; and when they do, they hardly read wide. So, it is believed that the African churches are a thousand miles wide but one inch deep. But of course, there are exceptions to every claim.

However, this couple saw themselves applying their purpose-intended life to solving the problems of the "ill-reading deficiency syndrome" and as an experiment they set up a pilot project to realize their dreams. It can be assumed that if one hid gold bars in books no black man in this part of the world might ever notice them.

So Mike and Evelyn opened the Trinity Bookshop, and to me it's a great vision with multiple obstacles. But to them, the obstacles were not deterrent forces to stop their vision. They believed Brescia didn't need new churches, though new ones would emerge. Brescia, in particular, and Italy, in general, need information and bookshops. They believed this would build the churches more than new pastors and new churches.

As Africans in the diaspora, at least their initial patronage should be their own. But unfortunately, most people hardly know where this resource center is situated. Even some pastors laugh to scorn when they get information about the dream because they don't see as they see. Mike and Evelyn's burden has paid off so much, however, and others are now emulating their example. Visionaries always locate a burden and they apply their lives to the solutions to the needs.

Visionaries Are Often Misunderstood

You see, my dear good reader, because of what one sees people will misunderstand the visionary before they will understand him. Probably, one day they will understand. They will understand his dream at the peril of their own weaknesses because of their disbeliefs. They will see it with their eyes but they will not be partakers of this divine blessing.

People must avoid the purpose-driven vision in order to embrace it later. By the time they see what one has seen, one is far ahead into seeing other positive achievements and this will always baffle them. God calls and makes visionaries wonderful signposts to the blind (see Isaiah 8:18).

Visionaries See and Prophesy, "By This Time Tomorrow"

In 2 Kings 6:24-25, the Syrians besieged Samaria and it led to national famine. Any time Israel despised the Lord, He allowed enemy invasions. This particular one was of such tragic dimensions. The famine was so severe that a donkey's head was as expensive as eighty shekels of silver; dove dung was also sold for money. Cannibalism emerged as a result. But in chapter 7, the prophet Elisha shows up with a prophetic solution. He openly confessed what he saw. He saw abundance and miraculous prosperity the following morning. He saw and prophesied, "By this time tomorrow" (2 Kings 7:1b NLT).

He went on to say that "by this time tomorrow" a seah of fine flour would be sold for a shekel and that two seahs of barley would be sold for a shekel (see 2 Kings 7:1). But the officer beside the king, who the king leaned on (adviser), laughed to scorn and said to the man of God, "That couldn't happen even if the LORD opened the windows of heaven!" (2 Kings 7:2b NLT). The truth of the matter was that Elisha (by faith) had manipulated legal time into spirit time. And he superimposed legal time with faith-divine time where everything is possible with God.

The answer the prophet gave to the natural thinker is worth considering: "You will see it happen with your own eyes, but you won't be able to eat any of it!" (2 Kings 7:2c NLT). Verses 17-20 reveal that the officer saw the provisions, but he was trampled to death at the gate. What we see is what we get; hence, we should always endeavor to see in the light of God's eyes.

Where one locates the provision equally determines where one will go and take the provision. If a person sees blessing in the spirit, for example, that same blessing will come from the spirit and manifest in the person's life in reality. So you see, we must see what we want (to get) and manipulate spirit time into our legal time frame and get it at once for breakthroughs. It will surely manifest.

VISIONARIES ARE OFTEN MISUNDERSTOOD BEFORE THEY ARE UNDERSTOOD

Now Philip was of Bethsaida, the city of Andrew and Peter. Philip findeth Nathanael, and saith unto him, We have found him, of whom Moses in the law, and the prophets, did write, Jesus of Nazareth, the son of Joseph. And Nathanael said unto him, Can there any good thing come out of Nazareth? Philip saith unto him, Come and see. Jesus saw Nathanael coming to him, and saith of him, Behold an Israelite indeed, in whom is no guile! Nathanael saith unto him, Whence knowest thou me? Jesus answered and said unto him, Before that Philip called thee, when thou wast under the fig tree, I saw thee. Nathanael answered and saith unto him, Rabbi, thou art the Son of God;

thou art the King of Israel. Jesus answered and said unto him, Because I said unto thee, I saw thee under the fig tree, believest thou? thou shalt see greater things than these. And he saith unto him, Verily, verily, I say unto you, Hereafter ye shall see heaven open, and the angels of God ascending and descending upon the Son of man.

—John 1:44-51 KJV

John 1:44-51 is a conversation of the voice of a visionary and a non-visionary. One major obstacle that great visionaries face is that they are often misunderstood before they may be understood. The life of Jesus and Nathanael depicts these particular claims. And the introduction of Nathanael by Philip and his subsequent response to the elevated gospel of Christ typifies the claims that visionaries are most often misunderstood in the beginning until they may be understood along the way if the right situations are applied.

The life of Philip reflects, deduces, and represents the typical voice of a man with vision who has newly caught a higher sense of revelation and elevation. His friend Nat was the opposite. He had human knowledge at its peak and it compartmentalized people based on external factors. One thing is always clear: a visionary is often misunderstood from the beginning and no matter how articulate he may be people misunderstand him.

Ordinary people give ordinary interpretations to life events; and normal interpretation is an affront to elevated thoughts. Ordinary thoughts cannot produce the consequential understanding required of a person to know God intimately. Visionaries are people who carry divine mandates and assignment purposes and they speak in an elevated thought because God is the producer of their understanding.

And so, doubts and traumas come from the fact that a visionary speaks, that one has logical proofs of who the visionary is or where he originates from, and that he can use his human thoughts to compartmentalize such a great gift and personality and impede the progress of the Kingdom. This is an obstacle to overcome and not succumb to.

However, one may have to be very careful because everybody can be somebody overnight. Everybody can discover purpose within a microsecond, have a change, and make a total turn around. Every doubter or sinner can turn 180 degrees and become a believer and righteous. The ordinary poor man down the road can be the next president and successful man in town. So, we should be careful of the way we treat people. We may not know what they may become one day.

We should be very careful not to classify and categorize men instantaneously and spontaneously. I believe that we hardly know who is the next man on God's spotlight of elevation; thus, we should be careful how we treat others. We must learn how to demonstrate the sweet fragrance of habits and ethical actions toward every person we meet down the lane because our success or failure is connected to the people we meet. How we treat people we meet, will determine how they will treat us in return when we meet them one day.

In relation to Christ Jesus's case, He was a carpenter, and at thirty years of age, He began His ministry as a prophet, teacher, and the Savior of the world. Who ever thought that was possible but Him? People saw Him as just a carpenter, a carpenter's son, but He saw Himself as the King and Savior of the world.

Overnight, He was recycled and redefined to conform to the image He saw. He got what He saw—that He was the Messiah—and no obstacle was effective to be erected against Him. You too can get anything you have seen and no erected obstacle or roadblock can impede and stop you. If only you will learn how to operate from the elevated sense, you can be whatever you see. Just begin to see it and you will get it.

In the records of John, we see Philip call out to his great friend Nathanael about the fact that he has seen the Christ and Messiah (whom the law and the prophets prophesied about). The response from Nathanael was "where does he come from?" The truth of the matter is that when people look at us based on race, education, culture, experience, age, gender, ability, disability, and groupings, they miss the mark of blessing. "Can any good thing come out of Nazareth?" (John 1:46a ASV). Sure it can! Why not? The Bible proves it.

Nathanael did not even take time to see the man before he talked. That is what self-made human intellectualism does. It rejects people before it witnesses them. It avoids and marginalizes high-elevated people with the excuse that "they are not our class—they are not from our tribe, race, country; they are women, men; they are too young, too old, too trained, not trained, and this and that, or they are men of color."

These types of knowledge and attitudes in humans have the seed of ignorance and arrogance as their hallmark and fame and it doesn't ensure our development whatsoever. This destructive weapon of religious civilization never allows humans to see the glory of God. For this reason, I say that it is an obstacle for "visionaries to be misunderstood before they are probably understood."

And the fact that people don't understand and appreciate the effort doesn't mean God has rejected the effort. Note that the stone that the builders rejected became the chief cornerstone for the entire building (see Psalms 118:22; Matthew 21:42b; Acts 4:11; 1 Peter 2:7b).

A PERSON IN WHOM THERE IS NO GUILE CAN ALSO BE ELEVATED TO SEE

In the said conversation, we see that Philip insisted and pulled his friend to the revelation and elevated seed. Christ Jesus was the elevated seed of Abraham through Israel; by Him the world will have salvation. So Philip most likely pushed his friend to the wall to come and see and stop talking like a Gentile; **come and see in the third-degree elevated sense, where the human assessment of people's origins isn't as important as their assignments and purposes.**

Philip might have said, "See this man and get great understanding." It seems one is still operating from the low-degree climate because one has not encountered the next elevated level of breakthroughs. Come and advance your thoughts through the Nazarene. He will change your paradigm thinking. And will Jesus really live up to the task? Will He prove His ministry according to the version Philip believed about Him?

Jesus saw him and said, "Behold an Israelite indeed, in whom is no guile!" (John 1:47b KJV). Jesus's answer shows the dimension of spiritual elevation and sense of purpose He carried. This purpose reconciles and does not impute the sins of men. The truth is that any high-sense elevated revelation doesn't ditch any person; instead, it elevates, builds, and strengthens. We see this in 2 Corinthians 5:18-19 (KJV): "And all things are of God, who hath reconciled us to himself by Jesus Christ, and hath given to us the ministry of reconciliation; To wit, that God was in Christ, reconciling the world unto himself, not imputing their trespasses unto them; and hath committed unto us the word of reconciliation."

The elevated spiritual sense rather serves as the basis for exaltation and upliftment. It sees the good side of people and not their bad side. It motivates people to get positive results and take them from the weak standpoints of human dungeons and covering to a spiritual standpoint of kingdom covering. It constructs and doesn't destroy. Jesus applauded the strength of Nathanael though he was under the fig tree (human covering and knowledge), "I saw thee." Then comes the shock of Nat's life. He then noticed his human nature, error, inadequacies, pride, and arrogance. He was suddenly humbled before the Lord and exclaimed, "Rabbi," meaning teacher.

Of course, friend, don't be shocked by this. But hang out with me and I will point and usher you to the God of Abraham, Isaac, and Jacob. You see, in reality every Jew believes in the high spiritual ranking of these great names mentioned above. The three were an epitome of God's relationship with mankind. Upon them was the covenant of promise built and defended. Abraham was the prophetic established covenant of blessing. He was the progenitor and protagonist of the God-man-faith relationship.

Isaac was the prophetic preservation of the covenant of promise. God said that He knew Abraham and that he (Abraham) would instruct the sons after him to observe His covenant and laws (see Genesis 18:19). Isaac initiated that. Jacob became the prophetic declaration and voice of the covenant of promise. The tribes of Israel emerged through Jacob with a spoken word and blessing for each one of them (see Genesis 49). Many times God introduced Himself to men uttering, "I am the God of Abraham, the God of Isaac, and the God of Jacob" (Matthew 22:31-32a)

REVELATION OPERATES VIA THE USE OF SYMBOLISM AND IT HELPS VISIONARIES TO OVERCOME OBSTACLES

How can one operate in the elevated sense of spiritual truth? He can tap and operate in spiritual matters through an elevated sense of revelation. Revelation comes through symbols and when one understands the unveiled aspect of the symbols, many keys can be released to open the doors of obstacles erected against his personal progress. God uses symbols a lot and your understanding of spiritual symbols can assist your journey of faith. Symbols can either appear in dreams or in reality and teach us privately about God, His relationships, His intentions, His judgments, His love, ways, and methods, His power, His Godhead, and many more. Joseph had a sense of purpose through dreams. Moses had a personal reality encounter through the burning bush experience and his authority to confront governmental powers was seen in the very rod he held.

It's imperative to remember that anytime an idea drops in one's mind it is a key of progress to solve mankind's problem. Also, an idea of doubt equally breeds on someone's mind to obstruct, distract, impede, block, prevent, and stop the dream from getting fulfilled. These are all obstacles. So for example, when the first plane landed as an idea on the minds of Wilbur and Orville Wright, the first doubt against their dream landed on the minds of experts and technical men to stop the fulfillment of the vision.

The reason for a series of articles by experts against the manufacturing of any plane was to prevent plane manufacturing on earth by nontechnical persons. So they wrote against the prolific idea, "There is no possible combination by which a metallic bird can fly." This was said in 1899. Two years later, in 1901, the Wright brothers manufactured the metallic bird. So you see, cynics and critics are everywhere in our world. We have just a few proactive people and woe to the person who is reactive; he will depend on circumstances and fail.

In this chapter, I have used the story of Nehemiah a lot because it has absolute resemblance to the present incidents in our generation. When Nehemiah began to build the broken wall, this is what Sanballat and Tobiah said out of anger and hatred, "What are these feeble Jews doing? Will they fortify themselves? Will they offer sacrifices? Will they complete it in a day? Will they revive the stones from the heaps of rubbish—stones that are burned? … Whatever they build, if even a fox goes up on it, he will break down their stone wall" (Nehemiah 4:2-3).

And mind you, the strength of one's enemy can grow because they can influence others to come in and mock the assignment in one's hands. I personally experienced mockery and scorn at the beginning, when I announced to people around me about the decision of engaging my capacity into active writing as my lifetime occupation.

Like with Nehemiah, immediately enemies were released against this great dream, but I overcame the obstacles. One's ability to overcome pressure to silence rising tongues against one's dream is a virtue we all must take seriously and develop. People want to see the success and wealth of a venture before they can commit their trust to it; however, great and wise men see the idea and they live to recognize and celebrate the dream.

The Sanballat-Tobiah-Geshem (STG) attitude is a resistance: a mockery spirit that is upgraded in every generation according to the pattern of human generations on the earth. This just means we have the same attitude in men who allow themselves as weapons and tools in the hands of the enemy.

Nehemiah 2:19 says, "But when Sanballat the Horonite, Tobiah the Ammonite official, and Geshem the Arab heard of it, they laughed at us and despised us, and said, 'What is this thing that you are doing? Will you rebel against the king?'"

But this was the true burden, responsibility, and assignment from God to a man. Every individual carries a special assignment mandate and because it varies from one another, public opinion about one's assignment may be detrimental. If it's not one's assignment, he hardly fancies and shows respect and admiration.

People hate and can fight with words, intending to destroy the work of our hands because God hasn't given them the same burden as others. Our passion may not interest the person immediately around us. But we shouldn't worry; we must be happy. That is, getting a negative reaction toward a dream should be classified as a part of normal and everyday life.

Also, when I announced my intention to become a minister of the gospel, the people who opposed me mostly were the ones very close to me at that time. They judged me as the "carpenter's son." They saw me as "the untutored disciple of Christ." Some saw me as a child, like Jeremiah. Others even criticized me, thinking I was becoming a fake prophet of this generation.

I have met people who pleaded with me because they felt guilty for what they once did. Even now some people call and ask for my forgiveness because of the part they played in a public scorn at one local church. When a human being doesn't believe God has called and assigned you, he will try to impede the progress of your life's assignments. But you must be temperate and teach everybody around you a timeless truth and lesson by saying, "Time will tell because time is the best teacher in life, so wait and see what the Lord can do with a person."

It's dangerous to look at one's stature and judge his or her abilities. The capacity of a thing is not seen in the structure but the engine. The engine capacity determines the spin and revolution of the thing. So one can be small, huge, short, or tall and the output will be determined by the input. As humans, our input is a result of our purposes.

Our purposes influence the input, the power wired in gifts and us as our potential. You see, it's not wise to allow another person to use your ignorance to gain an advantage and an edge over you. God created all human beings to be rulers and none of us should be dominated. The idea of lords and slaves came about as a result of our fall from the dominion realm.

Let me give a free advice: we do not need any of these destructive critics and cynics to endorse us before we can fulfill the vision, purpose, and leadership God has assigned to us. Even if they invite us for any conference, one shouldn't waste precious time and energy to attend, just like Nehemiah did.

Mostly, the invitation that comes from the camp of the enemy is meant to condition one to fail. So don't heed and respond. Nehemiah refused to sit with the wicked or stand in the way of the unrighteous or sit with those who scorned him. They sent more than four letters but he rejected their evil outbursts of wrath and conspiracies. He was above them:

> *Now it happened when Sanballat, Tobiah, Geshem the Arab, and the rest of our enemies heard that I had rebuilt the wall, and that there were no breaks left in it (though at that time I had not hung the doors in the gates), that Sanballat and Geshem sent to me, saying, "Come, let us meet together among the villages in the plain of Ono." But they thought to do me harm. So I sent messengers to them, saying, "I am doing a great work, so that I cannot come down. Why should the work cease while I leave it and go down to you?" But they sent me this message four times, and I answered them in the same manner. Then Sanballat sent his servant to me as before, the fifth time, with an open letter in his hand.* (Nehemiah 6:1-5)

What one sees is what God has revealed and he must believe and fulfill the purpose in what he sees. And never see what the enemy wants to condition the visionary to see. And even if what they see is the reality of a problem, see the problem as a big target for a bigger solution. This is what David saw as a youth before the battle of all ages was fought: between him and the dreadful Goliath, he saw the enemy beheaded (see 1 Samuel 17).

The great bulwark and opposition wasn't Goliath but Eliab—his own brother from the same household: "Now Eliab his oldest brother heard when he spoke to the men; and Eliab's anger was aroused against David, and he said, 'Why did you come down here? And with whom have you left those few sheep in the wilderness? I know your pride and the insolence of your heart, for you have come down to see the battle'" (1 Samuel 17:28).

Oftentimes, it seems that our own blood brother and friend fights our progress and not necessarily our enemy. Your enemy is just waiting to make you more popular and famous. You are about to be recognized and celebrated. David didn't really come just to see the battle, he came to kill the giant because he saw how God saw Goliath—a man who cannot defile the name of the Lord.

And because of what he saw, which others didn't, they weren't ready to listen to the version he carried. Yet, he kept on until he was able to persuade the officers at the battlefront. This lesson reveals that we too can certainly meet those who are designed to listen to us with rapt attention and see what we see. Eventually, they will sing a song for us and make us more popular very soon.

Finally, when the wall was completed, we discovered that the enemies of the vision then realized and saw what Nehemiah saw years ago: "So the wall was finished…And it happened, when all our enemies heard of it, and all the nations around us saw these things, that they were very disheartened in their own eyes; for they perceived that this work was done by our God" (Nehemiah 6:15-16).

God is all you need and His grace is sufficient to see you through to the top. He is the source of your vision, so keep in touch with Him and walk in His footsteps. As you succeed in your vision, some men will say, "Well, who knows the godfather behind his success?" They will say you are biting more than you can chew. Every visionary at a point in time may have been accused as being proud. Most men easily misinterpret one's vision-mission and gifts to mean pride.

The law of vision puts visionaries on a mission—a mission to action and inaction of some sort, which is most often than not considered as arrogance by natural sensors. People who operate on the scale of humanistic intelligence always have problems with great visionaries who operate from the elevated revelation level of intelligence. Visionaries tap into higher thoughts and higher ways. Consider Isaiah 55:7-11 (KJV):

Let the wicked forsake his way, and the unrighteous man his thoughts: and let him return unto the LORD, and he will have mercy upon him; and to our God, for he will abundantly pardon. For my thoughts are not your thoughts, neither are your ways my ways, saith the LORD. For as the heavens are higher than the earth, so are my ways higher than your ways, and my thoughts than your thoughts. For as the rain cometh down, and the snow from heaven, and returneth not thither, but watereth the earth, and maketh it bring forth and bud, that it may give seed to the sower, and bread to the eater: So shall my word be that goeth forth out of my mouth: it shall not return unto me void, but it shall accomplish that which I please, and it shall prosper in the thing whereto I sent it.

And as a visionary taps into a higher dimension of thought, a powerful action can emerge and all those people who wished him well will rejoice with him and congratulate him for making it. He made it because he understood the concept of right thoughts and better ways of God. So, God blesses his ways and thoughts and he prospers. We must note that God never said we can't have His ways or His thoughts. We can have His ways and thoughts as ours through a conscious effort to surrender totally unto Him.

So we must drop our own thoughts and ways and stick to God's thoughts and ways. This guarantees the success of our visions. One must not give his or her enemies the opportunity to claim they are his or her secret intercessors and mediators. God is always behind our achievements and accomplishments. That is why we need to depend solely on Him, who alone knows how far we have come and all that we have invested behind the scenes in what is now visible for all to see.

Also, you have a personal effort to make it happen. God's effort is the provision of the vision and your effort is the execution of the vision. It's reported by experts that today's people want an instant lifestyle. How true this is! They hate to know and understand the ways and processes through which things are made. So they always know the delicious recipes, but they are ignorant of the know-how. Thus, people lack knowledge on how their most favorite recipes are prepared.

For example, the best part of life is the knowledge on how to catch a fish from the pool and prepare it by oneself. The tastes of marine recipes might not be the best but the blessing of their preparation is. One is handicapped if one can enjoy something without knowing the way it came about. Our personal effort to make our vision manifest is the readiness to go through a state of processing to become refined and defined.

This can be likened to the process of creating products, which helps to give a wonderful packaging result. For instance, the end result of a long period of studies can be book writing. It can be inferred that the end result of any reasonable human effort can be seen in what he or she can produce and accomplish in his or her lifetime.

Let's consider or liken the issue to the drab cereal as an example; it is nothing more than processed grain of corn. In Europe, we spend billions of euros on it every year and this is because of its importance to our daily dieting and probably due to how it has been packaged and delivered on the shelves of supermarkets.

One is easily attracted to these products due to their processing and attractive packaging. It's reported that people buy things based on how they are presented. So proximity to products isn't the issue now; rather, how products are packed and sold. One must package one's gifts and talents before we market them to the world.

Therefore, as a visionary one must spend quality time in preparing one's self during important assignments though we may use less time in delivering what we have used endless hours mastering. As a public speaker, I have discovered an amazing secret significant for every human development: one must speak for a few minutes when called upon to deliver an impact-oriented message.

And such persons must prepare for hours in order to make the required impact expected of him or her. I prepare myself for hours to be efficient and effective. We spend brief moments with our audience and yet we must give them what they need. What we deliver as public officers showcases how well or ill-prepared we are.

Be it as it may be, the success or failure of our vision is equally in our hands as much as it is in the hands of God. This reveals the importance of the biblical passage, which states that "without Me you can do nothing" (John 15:5c). In principle, God needs us in order to succeed in our vision and equally we need God to help us fulfill our vision since He is the source and origin of every vision on earth. You don't need the prototype Sanballats, Tobiahs, and Geshems to accomplish what you see.

And you neither need Eliab though he is your blood brother. They are distorters of dreams, blockers of vision, impediments to direction, distracters of ways and methods, enemies of progress, and goalkeepers to your goals. The only person highly unavoidable in your life is the source of your life and He is God. This makes the words of our Lord Jesus Christ relevant: "Without Me you can do nothing" (John 15:5c); and also His words stating, "With God all things are possible" (Matthew 19:26c). And "all things" includes what you see—your vision.

The time you make for your vision, that is, the efforts you make through constant, diligent attitudes, and to crown it all, your relationship with your Creator, who is "the **author and finisher** of our faith" (Hebrews 12:2a), plays a major role in employing all the powers of your imagination. Persevere in faith and action until your dream is realized.

When Nehemiah heard about the condition of the remnants in Jerusalem, the Bible says that he had a burden for restoring the image of Jerusalem. He might have risen up to the task. But the Bible unveils a powerful secret. According to the records, Nehemiah fasted and prayed.

There were kinds of circumstances he needed in fasting to buttress home results. Nehemiah 1:4-11 state,

So it was, when I heard these words, that I sat down and wept, and mourned for many days; I was fasting and praying before the God of heaven... "O great and awesome God, You who keep Your covenant and mercy with those who love You and observe Your commandments...be attentive and Your eyes open...hear the prayer of Your servant which I pray before You now, day and night...and confess the sins of the children of Israel which we have sinned against You. Both my father's house and I have sinned....let your servant prosper this day, I pray, and grant him mercy in the sight of this man." For I was the king's cupbearer.

THE WORLD IS DIVIDED BETWEEN THE FAILURES AND THE SUCCESSFUL

Normally, society can be divided into two separate categories. There are those who succeed and those who fail. Those who fail may not necessarily be less intelligent, experienced, and less godly than those who succeed. It is believed that those who fail don't see opportunities at the right time; though they may be at the right places at the wrong time.

Sometimes, the thin difference between those who succeed and those who fail can be attributed to their God-given vision and their ability to see and use opportunities. They are failures probably, due to their over-dependence on themselves instead of God.

Visionaries depend on their God-enhanced wisdom and pay less attention to human abilities. Those who fail seem to trust so much in the "chariots" of the strengths of their temperament, their credentials, social standing, and human connections, and often neglect how diligent one must be in seeking the will of God. No wonder they fail miserably.

In my life, I have seen how some people started and it seemed they were doing very well. And suddenly they fail and fade away like the morning dew. When one goes deep down to find out why they suddenly fell, you will discover to one's amazement that those people lived without respecting God.

WE EMBRACE THE WILL OF GOD FOR OUR OWN VISION SUCCESS

In as much as we need to have vision and hard work with focused attitude and persistence, we should not forget about the God-factor. One must "see God" and seek His help before he can properly see any image in his heart. When one sees the golden image in his vision pursuit, he must also endeavor to seek the mind of God for the accomplishing of the very vision.

We should remain so faithful to God, for He is the Source of all true visions and the omniscient One who knows the end of our dreams. When we commit our dreams to Him, like Joseph, He will guide us through all the difficulties and see to it that our vision speaks to the end. By His transforming power, He turns dreams and visions into realities. He makes today's impossibilities become tomorrow's miracles. He turns our vision-related trials and tests into living testimonies.

Dear reader, it is important to know that without God one can do nothing on his own and with God all things are possible. In the discovery and pursuit of one's vision, it's imperative to understand that one's unique and definite purpose manifests distinctively to make him or her a crucial factor in life. Just as the human fingers and traits are separate from each other, so are our visions (purposes) and hence, no person should waste his precious time and effort in fighting one another on the basis of competitions and conflicts. It's on this note that we fight one another through the battle of bad wishes rather than wills.

And we should be carriers of wills, intents, and purposes; not carriers of bad wishes and programs. It is equally sad to see people look for God's will, intent, and purpose everywhere apart from within themselves. So we must look within ourselves first, as we are the glorified version of God on earth, to discover what we must do as visionaries and purpose-oriented people.

Every type of progress in this world comes from God. We know that it's through God that everything emanates and He uses us human beings to channel His intentions on earth. God's benefits are distributed to people through visionaries who discover the intents, purposes, and wills of God on earth.

VISION IS SPECIFIC AND ITS GOALS MUST BE STRATEGIC

Every vision must be specific and must also have definite goals. One must note that every vision is God-created and given and its related principles bring strategic goals for the fulfillment of the dream. Vision is a development of the heart. For this reason, I am strongly advising that everyone must have a definite goal so that we achieve our individual visions and intentions.

I believe that if any person, group of people, or any association fails to have specific visions and goals in a formidable way, this indicates that such an organization will definitely not succeed. For this reason, I am advising every leader to struggle to know the importance and rudiments of strategic planning and vision. The fact is that each one is different and must think differently to do something different. For example, in our church, Messianic Temple, we are specific in our vision declaration. I have spelled it out clearly elsewhere in this book.

We train people to be leaders and we coach them specifically on how to be influential kingdom leaders who can affect society in every facet of life.

We do this to guide the church into becoming Word-based, spirit-filled and led. When we do this, then the rest of the assignment is left in the hands of the Holy Spirit for the growth and health of the ministry. So we have no struggles at all in society because we know the definite thing God has called us to do. This suggests to me that each one of us carries a definite assignment and we must struggle to fulfill it on earth.

When a person doesn't know his vision, he sets goals and organizes programs as vision. We shouldn't forget this: vision is always specific and definite and goals are strategic plans and they differ. If you want to sell clothes, for instance, you should be able to specify the exact materials you want to sell. A person who comes to me and says, "I want to deal in clothes has no vision."

You must be able to tell me the kinds of clothes you want to deal in. You should be able to tell me whether the clothes are meant for kids, adults, or for celebrities and even whether it will be unisex (gender neutral) or gender specific. This is a definite and precise vision and I can buy into it. When one's vision is clear, people then will know why one must be contacted and what people should get from one.

Many a time, I encounter many pastors and in the course of our conversations, I have had the opportunity of listening to their views on the issues. Some will say, "God has called me to reach out to my community," or "I have a vision to build a 55,000-capacity church." Please, don't ever confuse goals with missions, visions, and purposes, no matter how close they seem. Many people confuse vision and purpose, or vision and mission, or vision and goal. So some people consider their goals as their vision; this shouldn't be the case.

Purpose is the reason behind the existence of something. Vision is the direction through which a purposeful assignment can be realized; goals are the organized strategies through which one's purpose and vision can be accomplished. We all have missions as believers because we have been commissioned by the Lord to reach out to the world and propagate the gospel (see Matthew 28:18-20; Mark 16:15).

So our mission is to fulfill the great commission through our individual visions. One must be specific with where he's going to with the 55,000-dream congregation, else he may reach there and still feel empty because he couldn't point a specific direction for a purpose to be accomplished to 55,000 people.

GOD MUST BE THE CENTER OF THE VISION FOR US TO BE CENTRAL FIGURES OF THE VISION

God is the center of life and wisdom, while men are the central figure in life. Therefore, it is vital that one remains in God and finds out how his or her vision must be seen by society. When a visionary gives everything he has in this world for God, he will succeed. If one likes, he can carry the whole world on his chest and reject God and he will become a vagabond, fugitive, mesmerized delinquent, and a total failure. Until God assumes the center stage of all our visions, we may find it difficult to discover what we are looking for. God is the centrifugal custodian and giver of human visions while man is the central figure of all Heaven-intended visions and purposes.

If a visionary fails to take note of these underlying principles, all the things he does will be thwarted and failure will be his inevitable lot. Why? Because He is the One who gave and built in us the logic of purpose in the first place. In this case, I feel it's appropriate now to stop scratching our heads and minds for just a minute and invite God into your lives. Say this right now: **"Lord Jesus, please come into my life as the Savior of my life. Be Lord over me, my vision, and purpose. I surrender myself to You right now. Come into my life from today."**

You and I can do nothing on our own if we reject our Maker. Anything at all can impede our vision when we walk without God. God created us and He has the Master Plan for our existence on earth. He designed His Word (the Bible) as our manual—guide for effective living. Rejecting His Word equally means rejecting God.

If you have caught the revelation that without God you cannot do anything, then learn how to read the Bible, pray, and meditate about God every day in your life. Think of God before you think of life's successes. The true meaning of seeking God and His righteousness is the true meaning of all things being added to you (see Matthew 6:33).

GOD IS OUR CREATOR AND MAKER AND NOBODY CAN DO WITHOUT HIM. Dear reader, let's learn how to lean on God for one cannot do without Him. You need absolute faith in the God of your vision. He alone has what it takes to spot opportunities in dry and rough patches. He gives you the eye of an eagle and guides you to locate the hidden treasures of the earth. He can pick you from nowhere and plant you somewhere.

In this life, there are paths "which no fowl knoweth, and which the vulture's eye hath not seen" (Job 28:7 KJV). It takes the eyes (vision) of God who "cutteth out rivers among the rocks; and his eye seeth every precious thing….God understandeth the way thereof, and he knoweth the place thereof. For he looketh to the ends of the earth, and seeth under the whole heaven" (verses 10, 23-24).

VISION IS UNIVERSAL AND HAS NO LIMITATIONS

I want to appeal to my readers that wherever one finds himself or herself in life is a place to showcase one's vision, purpose, and life's assignments without allowing external limitations whatsoever.

Today, those of us from the so-called Third World have the belief that migrating to Europe or to the United States of America will ultimately help us to achieve our dreams and vision assignment.

> "Real faith is not the stuff dreams are made of; rather it is tough, practical, and altogether realistic. Faith sees the invisible but it does not see the non-existent."
>
> —*A. W. Tozer*

It seems as if once we enter any of these places, all roads lead to one's desired destination, but that is a mirage and the beginning of a struggle. Symbolically, Europe or none of the developed worlds are destinations in themselves. They may be channels through which one can get to his destination. Discovery of new horizons and geographical places can lead us to our ultimate purpose and destination if we can coordinate and connect to our Maker.

One must know what he or she is allotted with, a gift or potential, and this can equally help him or her to identify the geographical location he or she must live in, so that one's gift, talent, and potential puts him on demand to travel and not vice versa.

Purpose determines and influences where one ought to be and not necessarily people's external factors and circumstances. For example, if you discover yourself in a place, the true meaning in God's mind can be that you have what it takes to influence that particular place with what you have. Change is a constant factor and wise men use its power to turn things positively.

Do you know that it is not everyone living in the Western world or other parts of the earth that succeed in life? Where one is located is not as important as what God wants him or her to be. For example, I know of many people who have stayed many years in some of these parts of the world without some tangible results. Does this mean that they missed their individuality and purpose?

All they struggled for comes to nothing in spite of their candid efforts. Regrettably, after all these years of efforts, they relocate back home without anything to show for it. On the other hand, record has it that some of these so-called failed people who have relocated from the Western world sometimes become big, rich, and wealthier in their new-found homes. What can be the reason for this new circumstance? The answer is in our minds. The answer is found in the wind.

This suggests that whether we live in an economically developed nation or in a less developed nation or whether we are an individual doesn't guarantee success. Where we live can easily become our own obstacle to progress when we refuse to consider the importance of our relationship to God's intended purposes and assignments. One must take time to find where God wants him or her to be at any time. And most of the events recorded in the Bible came as a result of a need to fortify mankind.

Thus, let's relate this to an economic analogy on the production and consumption of goods and services. In economic terms, the risk act of production isn't based or limited to anybody in any place.

The act of producing any particular product is based on the visionary's ability to know exactly what is in demand anywhere.

Then, we can say that a positive-thinking visionary is somebody who knows what the world's markets demand from manufacturers and he relates to it for his success. That is to say, a businessman or trader can lose profits and incur debts if he will not consider the market patterns and invest appropriately and vice versa.

Visions are fulfilled because God is the One who inspires them everywhere. Any visionary who is without faith in God can be limited. Every visionary needs hard work and discipline to succeed, and failure to apply these principles will surely result in failure no matter where the person is domiciled whether in the remote jungles of the world or in the cities of New York.

One must consider the logical principles of vision for his success. So, hard work, self-discipline, and candid efforts combine with God's intended vision and purpose to yield inevitable results. God should be the center of what you see else what you see becomes an obstacle in itself everywhere.

FAILURE IS INEVITABLE WHEN MEN LIVE OUTSIDE GOD'S DIRECTION

God created the earth for man to harness, subdue, and control. It is vividly stipulated in Genesis 1:28 that man must have dominion over the earth. God's purpose for creating the earth was for two major reasons: the first reason is to have **purpose of relationship** with man and all creation; the second reason is that He wants humans to have **purpose of vocation**. We are supposed to dress and keep (decorate and maintain) the earth from all external contaminations. When we live to fulfill our original purposes for creation, we reap abundantly and prosper (see Genesis 1:26-31; 2:7-17).

However, if we walk in darkness without our visions centered on Him we may not be able to achieve the aforementioned. So in order to succeed and realize our God-given visions and purposes, we must be faithful to God. Therefore, unfaithfulness on the part of a visionary becomes one of the major obstacles against his personal development and success orientation. Faith can help erase other existing obstacles in positive seeing experiences.

WHAT VISION ARE YOU PURSUING AT THE MOMENT?

DO YOU HAVE A VISION FOR YOUR PERSONAL LIFE? If you do, can you specifically and explicitly put your vision on paper now? An ardent adherent of a vision should be able to produce four or five statements that vividly portray and clarify his vision and dream without mincing words. Everything one sees around him or her occurred because somebody had an idea and was able to act boldly on his or her desired dreams.

Every vision must be written down somewhere. Every vision has to have a statement on records to avoid human errors. As an individual, what vision do you have for yourself and family? Write it down and act on it now. Rhema Williams believes that "nothing can be invented in this world just by thinking alone. An act must buttress the thinking."

What is your vision as a member of a local church if you are a believer? Do you have a vision for your business and every other thing around you? How much money do you expect or anticipate possessing one day? In spite of what your opinion may be, it's important that you constantly pray over it until it's achieved. And one can be effective in his vision application when he learns how to develop a written version of the thought. You can even write down the anticipated amount in a check and put it down somewhere you can see until you are able to "claim it."

One must always remember that the power of life and death, prosperity and poverty, righteousness and unrighteousness, good and bad, wisdom and foolishness lies on our own tongue and what arousal one gets determines the virtue or vice that comes out of him. Thus, we can say what we desire according to the intent of God so that it can be accomplished. God knows every situation that confronts us.

Therefore, it is vital that we refrain from saying things based on how we feel. Instead, we must confess the Word of God over our circumstances. We must learn how to speak up a language significant in the position related to our vision and purpose because without it we can fail. Those who succeed in life always plan to succeed.

There are no vacuums for jokes around people who succeed. Hence, let me ask: Are your visions positive or negative? Are you living day-by-day and night-by-night just taking whatsoever comes your way? Are you proactive and the articulate type or the reactive, inarticulate individual? Have you counted the cost of pursuing and fulfilling your life's visions? Answer all these on paper. It will help.

You can ignite divine passion that can propel you to move ahead. Passion and enthusiasm are common phenomena with great visionaries. One can inflict pain as an obstacle or impediment, but the passionate visionary will use enthusiasm and passion to ride over the evil. A visionary pursues excellence. And the proof of mediocrity in a person is the despising and resentment of excellence and perfection.

May you never be like those that put their trust in their "chariots" and in their "horses" (achievements and accomplishments). May you cease to rely on your bows and arrows—qualifications, personality, gifts, talents, wealth, experience, social contacts (strengths). These are means God may choose to use or ignore; but following the God of destiny must be one's focus. May you trust in Jehovah and be like Mount Zion, which can never be moved. May you cease to be chicken and begin to mount wings like the eagle. We have to learn how to soar at all cost so that we can fly past all the impediments on our way and fulfill our God-inspired vision.

The confusion we face as obstacles now may be adduced to the following reasons:

1. Lack of vision
2. Non-adherence to the process of vision principles

3. Wrong, hasty, and malnourished attitudes of a person with a quality vision

4. Procrastinations and complacencies in vision-oriented persons

5. Selfishness and ignorance

6. Illness and ill health, among other factors

WISDOM WORD

"I need to impress upon both male and female that is necessary for a male to have a vision for himself, his family, and all those under his influence. He must have a vision, for he was created to be a visionary."

—Dr. Myles Munroe

Chapter 6

TAKE THESE STEPS AND ACTUALIZE WHAT YOU SEE

Visions do not "just happen." They only come to pass when a person hears a word from God, harnesses it in his heart, speaks it, obeys it, and works toward the fulfillment of it with all the energy he has; spirit, soul, and body. When God speaks His Word to you and gives you a vision, He also says, "Work! For I Am with you."
—Guy Duininck

Hearing and seeing or vice versa, determines and influences beliefs. And it is beliefs and not benefits that motivate people to act. We humans are motivated by what we believe. You can win the bout against failure if you dare to believe. If one fails to develop his faith, his doubts will develop him or her. It is not the wrong you have done, it is not what society scrutinizes with their punitive judgments, it is your beliefs and acts that conquer impossibilities.

Belief creates emotional feelings that create confession or verbalization, which in a sense is an action. We must learn to say what we believe and believe in what we say. We must always say what we see by making references like "I think," "I suggest," "I feel," and "it is this or that." Verbalization determines and increases habit-action. Your actions create your circumstances and consequences. As a human being, you only have strong power to control your habits and ethical actions, but not the consequences of your actions.

Yes, you can throw yourself at the car because of wrath, but you cannot determine and reverse the consequences of the pains that you will suffer as a result of that action. This pain is always found in place of regret because you hurt. The other pain, that of discipline, brings out the consequence of a better life. You can stop your actions but you cannot stop the consequences of your own actions. Can you? You can throw yourself against a moving object, but you cannot stop yourself from hurting or dying as a result. Who cares? Maybe Superman, Rambo, and Chuck Norris. They can do such things in fictional stories. But in reality, men such as Chuck Norris are more careful than many others because they want to live long and enjoy their wealth.

Seeing is an action and the result one gets from how one sees is crucial. Habit-actions are always the steps we have chosen for ourselves. As a preacher, I persuade people that the skill of seeing must be taught, no matter the natural intrinsic instinct of seeing we possess. Every discipline of life needs some form of training and coaching. It bothers me a lot when I see people engage in the science of seeing without an iota of understanding. Gaining mastery or not in the art of seeing has resulted in the light of circumstances we find ourselves in.

Note that it is always better to see and get revelations and a sense of elevation. In the days of King David's dynasty, the Cushite saw and reported, but Ahimaaz heard and reported. So both ran; but one ran with the right message and the other just reported what he was told (see 2 Samuel 18:19-32).

Inventors master their eyes on their inventions; therefore, they bless us with the gift and talent of invention. They will hide themselves for ages and come out with what they have seen over the years. You see, people who see what they report are often more accurate in disseminating information than those who are informed. I want to see and not just be informed. When I hear something, I must verify what I heard by cross-checking. This is the right biblical Berea example (Acts 17:10-11 KJV):

And the brethren immediately sent away Paul and Silas by night unto Berea: who coming thither went into the synagogue of the Jews. These were more noble than those in Thessalonica, in that they received the word with all readiness of mind, and searched the scriptures daily, whether those things were so.

When we are not witnesses to an issue, people can easily misinform us. If you refer this discussion to the issues in a court of justice, there should always be clear evidence or witnesses to process a case and not hearsay or rumors. The aforementioned are prerequisites in deciding a case in the justice system; and so it is in the Kingdom of God. The church demands leaders who can witness evidently a relationship with the Lord and also see Him like Isaiah the prophet (see Isaiah 6:1, 5c). The art, act, and mastering of seeing can be categorized in the evidence group of assessment, which the visionary must know.

The subject—vision is the art, act, and mastering skill of seeing— readily brings to our minds the conversation between prophet Habakkuk and the Almighty God. The prophet was sent by God as a "watchman" to prophesy to Judah concerning an impending invasion by the Chaldeans (see Habakkuk 1:5-6).

At that time, the Jews were experiencing a time of moral and spiritual decline. God revealed to the prophet that He was using Babylon as a rod of correction against His own people and Habakkuk became perplexed and burdened. As he mused over God's prophetic declarations, this was what the prophet said, touching on the subject of vision, "I will stand at my watch and station myself on the ramparts; I will look to see what he will say to me, and what answer I am to give to this complaint" (Habakkuk 2:1 NIV).

This story is very significant to our subject of study in relation to discovering our vision or purpose in life. To catch a vision of purpose or have a revelation from God, we must strategically position ourselves at the right places and at the right times, with the right attitude and aptitude. Receiving divine revelation or impartation is subject to obedience and not disobedience. Habakkuk had positioned himself well in obeying God, though the entire nation had gone astray from God. And because of his right behavior God answered his "complaint" as is seen in verses 2-3 (KJV): "And the LORD answered me, and said, Write the vision, and make it plain upon tables, that he may run that readeth it. For the vision is yet for an appointed time, but at the end it shall speak, and not lie: though it tarry, wait for it; because it will surely come, it will not tarry."

God's answer to Habakkuk is a major universal principle on vision that transcends time. We can therefore apply it in our bid to capture and fulfill our visions from God. Out of this Scripture, I want us to take a look at six basic steps we need whenever we have a vision and desire to fulfill it effectively and in line with God's will. It may look as if the act of writing our vision and purpose has already been discussed. Yes! But we can cement the lessons in diverse ways to make a radical turn around for success. Every vision has six basic steps to follow according to prophet Habakkuk.

> **Step One:** The vision must be in a written form. Write the vision and give it a long-term plan.
>
> **Step Two:** The vision must be clear. Make the vision plain.
>
> **Step Three:** The vision must attract a synergic force around it. We must call men to the table.
>
> **Step Four:** We must learn how to move our vision to action. We must run the vision.
>
> **Step Five:** We must learn to wait for the vision's fulfillment.
>
> **Step Six:** The vision will surely come to pass because it has a time frame.

Every God-oriented vision must be written down because it carries the seed of elevation. One must equally know that anything that elevates humans must be documented. Then, a plan must be developed in order to realize the dreams of the thing. For instance, if all the potential treasures of dead humans in the cemetery could be tapped and used, the inevitable successes for man would be overwhelming.

But we can't have these lost treasures, so we must initiate and build capacity to salvage all treasures in humans before their death. And the key to doing this is in our ability to write our visions and goals strategically and implement them over time. After all, it's believed that everything comes if only one can wait and nothing obstructs the human will.

One must know that vision is the best legacy a person can inherit. That is why it must be documented. The greatest inheritance one can leave for posterity is not of material gains but of written and documented directions in life. It is good to possess functioning eyes, but it is best to possess hearty functioning of the heart because the heart attracts visions.

Vision is the unveiling of a thing, which comes in an imaginative picture. The thing was there and it is revealed now. It existed but wasn't seen and it is now made known. Vision brings light and revelations in picture forms and we as visionaries recycle the pictures into written forms in order to get better interpretations and consequences. This means that we can walk vision steps when they are written.

For example, Moses held a staff for many years until he had the burning bush experience. It was upon the experience that the authority of the rod was revealed. The rod was authoritative before the experience. But Moses saw its authority in the light of controlling sheep and not governments.

The other side of nature was the spirit sense and he could only be operative in there after the miraculous encounter. God gives us miracles in order for us to generate faith in what we already possess. Miracles are pointers and not the pointed. There is something in your hands meant for something you have not known yet and if you will seek and find out, you will become a great authority on earth.

It's vital to know this: God never gives us anything new on earth apart from the revelations of what we have in Him (see Galatians 1:15-16). We already possess everything that will make us fulfill our purpose before we came to the earth. The greatest setback is our inability to discover, know, and understand what we possess. So God will always bring a miracle our way in order to create the awareness; and He will again use the awareness to bring us to what we have that conquers the world.

Seeing is the act of revelation and revelation is the seed for human discovery, which leads to elevations. Faith is the ingredient God issues to our hearts when a miracle is performed so that we can see rightly. Moses believed God immediately after the encounter, such that he was prepared to face his ancient enemy—the pharaoh of Egypt.

The burning-bush experience generated faith in Moses to believe that the rod was an apostolic authority for the confrontations of governments and nations on earth. Until then, it was a staff controlling the mammalian kingdom. We need positive vision and every single situation can be celebrated as purpose fulfillment when they fall in line with the will, intent, and purpose of God. I believe we need awareness more than anything else. One's leadership authentication is in the fulfillment of his or her vision, which comes by awareness and not ignorance.

We must learn how to create vision billboards and not just "build castles in the air" about the uniqueness of our vision. This may be tantamount to boasting, which has no place in the Kingdom of God. You need to put down those "mental movies" on paper and confess them always. This skill ensures and guarantees fulfillment. For instance, if you want to attain a degree, then you have to write down practical steps (starting from today) as to how you are going to start and end the course.

It is believed that you can drive from where you know to the unknown. You can start with what you have, to reach what you don't have. Therefore, we can liken this to a road map, which gives direction and keeps us on track to get to our destination from where we started. So as our vision, it directs and organizes us to the end. Written vision is like a road map. You will never get lost on the way to your dream world. No matter how retentive one's IQ and memory may be, he or she must learn how to write down the vision. This is because one's memory can deceive him. Know that in life "what is written is written." And God watches over what is written to act on our behalf.

We are in the information age and thanks to the personal computer (PC) this is possible. With the help of the computer, one can record every detail of his vision and store it for future reference. Currently, the PC I am using is five years old. This means it has written records that are five years old. All this important information can be reached just by a click. But if I had kept them in my mind, guess for yourself!

Data keeping makes one just a click away from recalling his God-given vision. Each day, a person can open his or her laptop or PC anytime and read over the vision and as he or she does so, he or she will be inspired to work diligently and pray fervently until it is time to implement the vision. As one does so, the Almighty God, whose joy is always to see us succeed, will support him or her in all undertakings toward the realization of the vision.

Do Not Ever Fail to Document the Vision God Has Given You

Many have failed today because of lack of vision, while there are others who have vision but have failed because they failed to record their visions and have forgotten what the whole vision was about. Thus, an individual who fails to document the vision is equal to the person who has no vision. It seems to me that people may have similar ideas in a day, but some people seem more serious in their implementation than others.

People with no written versions of their intended goals and visions fail. They had no reference points without written records though they needed it most, so they failed. How serious you become about the idea that runs through your mind determines and influences what action you will take and ultimately the consequence.

Your reference point is the documented vision and your strategic vision plan is like a map that directs you to the desired destination. The compass of your purpose is your vision. The written vision is the code and key that helps to actualize human purposes.

If you live without a documented vision, you have become like the unwise virgins who did not have enough fuel to wait for their bridegroom. In search of the virgins with oil (the wise virgins), the bridegroom came in for the wedding ceremony and the unwise virgins were left out (see Matthew 25:1-12). Document your vision and stay with it all the time. Let it be as the Torah, printed on the forehead and recited as a poet rehearses his poetic stanzas.

Your Ability to Know and See Your Future before the Time Is a Vision Virtue

The end of a vision must begin from its inception. God had the end in view before He started creation. This explains His title name—Alpha and Omega. Architects know the end of their projects before they begin. Artists finish their artwork before they start. The maker knows the end of a thing.

Spectators fancy the end, which was well known to the manufacturer. We must look at the end of everything from the beginning and the beginning from the end. Every visionary has the ability to look at the whole vision before the vision begins, and he can confidently dictate the direction to the end from the beginning.

For instance, the United Kingdom—as in many other developed nations—already has the outlook of what the city of London will be like in the year 2030. You too can visualize your outlook in 2020 and trust God to get you there. Dare and see the office complex and the staff members coming down the aisles. See the reality of the supermarket dream with thousands of inflows.

You can see the fleet of ships and planes in your worldwide transportation business. The miracle of seeing through produces getting through. So see yourself sitting with people who matter and are current players in the assignment. See the church go multifaceted in ministry. And if you aren't married yet, see yourself married to the handsome-looking figure with 100 percent character traits. See something and get something. If you see nothing, you can have nothing and if you see something, you get something. There is blessing in the power of positive seeing. No seed no fruit and so forth and so on.

You must determine your success outfit before you can get it as such. If for instance, cities of the nations are planned way ahead of time then you too can plan way ahead of time and get it. The town and city planners have put all their plans down on paper and they are passed on from generation to generation. The document of development is kept as a reference point for development. This is what we call vision, seeing ahead and preparing for what you see ahead. Vision is in the imaginative and it is related to the future. The documented version enables you to set goals for the vision.

The human mind has three important functions—mental memories of things in the past, mental records of present issues (current affairs), and mental projections of future imaginative issues. You must understand the major dynamics of the mind and use it to get what you see. Decide that you will see something from now and get what you see in the future.

Your Written Vision Must Be Accompanied by a Long-Term Plan

As much as documented vision is good, it becomes better when you go further to develop a plan of action concerning how you want that vision implemented. The nations that are called "developed world" today did not appear developed overnight. No, the governments and citizens toiled and stayed long nights when their counterparts in less-developed or developing nations were lavishly sleeping the nights away.

The fact is, if you sleep for eight hours every day and you live up to seventy-five years, you have used twenty-five years of your lifetime just sleeping. The individual who sits and eats three square meals every day (assuming each meal takes one hour) after 75 years has spent approximately 9 good years of his entire life on earth eating. So then, the argument is, if you lived 75 years and ate meals that took nine years of your life and also slept 25 years (8 hours a day), you in reality lived for about 40 years. Unfortunately, the adage says that "true life begins at 40." So you didn't actually live on earth, you entered and left just like probably an aborted fetus.

As the popular adage goes, "Rome was not built in a day," it is also said that "when you come to Rome do what the Romans do." These statements originated as a result of the fact that Rome has been built on a vision that made it an international tourist center today. For example, Michael Angelo's cistern temples of paintings alone attract millions of tourists every year. It took several years of progressive developments by various successive governments to realize that dream. They were all built according to and on the visions of their forebearers.

The positive programs and support in Italian society inspired me and it helps me to create a positive mental picture of the future, which I desire as a heritage for my children and posterity. One common lesson can be learned when one visits Italy and that is the spirit of laughter. The early Italians had a definite idea and belief and it is represented in the folk tales, that laughter is therapeutic in value and even that the only cure for melancholy is laughter. Wow!

I assure you that the greatest form of inheritance is the one we leave in our children and not what we leave for them. The eternal values and godly mental heritage we develop in them is what they will utilize tomorrow to light their own visions, move progressively forward, and develop into what God has designed them to be.

I urge that we deposit knowledge in the world and project wisdom to the ends of the world. The Greeks have stocked our world with rich deposits of wisdom and we all depend on them for the advancement of the human age. This must be the equal portion of today's visionary and it is for our children's children.

You Must See Your Vision as a
Seed That You Have Planted

This seed when planted needs manure and attention for it to grow and bear fruits. If you refuse to take care of the seed by neglecting to weed and fail to apply the necessary manure, the seed will not bear enough fruits and sometimes no fruit at all, but wither away. So in order to realize your vision, you must undertake long-term planning.

One way of planning the future is to use the benefits of hindsight. Know what didn't work in history and eliminate it if it will not work for you in the future.

In Jesus's generation, He saw that the fig tree would not produce the desired results, so Christ eliminated it. The account is revealed as Jesus walked with His disciples and saw a fig tree, which was without fruit; He cursed it out of existence (see Mark 11:12-14, 20-21). Of course, the history of the fig had always produced leaves way back in the Garden of Eden. The fig had a long history of unproductivity and therefore it could not just use manure and water relevant for productive sectors in the field of agro-economy.

The fig, as unproductive as it was, also shielded humans symbolically and gave them alternative protection in God's eyes. It served as human covering after we rebelled against God in Eden (see Genesis 3:7b). Jesus was then dealing with an ancient root issue and knowledge that man depended on. When man has something to depend on, he refuses and rejects God because he has a temporal shelter. So Jesus destroyed the roots of our natural reliance and revealed to us the weakness of our beliefs so that we can depend on God who is our true source and protection.

Time Is Very Essential for Our Vision to Materialize

Relate your vision to time and be patient. The test of one's patience is the instruction to wait. Thus, as you are instructed to wait, patience doesn't only stifle your action steps, but it also tests the efficiency of your ethical habit. Do not be in a hurry, for there is no hurry in life. A pastor friend once said, "If you rush in life, you will get rashes." God has a set time for all His children who dwell on the face of the earth. This is the reason behind the great statements in the Bible such as, "There is a time for everything…under the heavens….He has made everything beautiful in its time" (Ecclesiastes 3:1-11a NIV).

God lives in eternity time zone whereby the past, the present, and the future are before Him. He then injects purpose and vision from the operable spirit time to the sun time and man applies his energy to these Heaven-assigned principles by obedience and understanding of them. God brings every vision to successful realization every time and we enjoy the benefits of the action. This means that vision-like purpose generates from God and starts from you on earth.

Remember, our Lord Jesus manifested Himself to the world at the time His Father wanted Him to. Heaven observes time because God relates to men to fulfill a purpose for men on earth. And every single revelation from God is a time to engage us to fulfill one's purpose without considering obstacles related to natural phenomena. God will never visit any person unless there's a reason for it. Any decision of God in Heaven for the earth gets manifested by time through a chosen vessel.

You can rise to another level because there is the elevation to another level in whatever one does. When the visionary masters a level in his calling and assignment, the door to another level opens for him. There's always something above you and mastering what is under the feet, becomes the platform for another level that is above. This means there is a dimension above, which one must be ready to rise up to at every point in time, no matter how big he becomes.

There Is a Rising Storm for Every Level Above Us

Between the period of the vision and the period the thought gets fulfilled is the emergence of a type of invisible storm. We go through storms every day in dimensional degrees and they may be positive or negative to determine the climatic condition afterward. Take the climate for example; there is time for the dry and rainy seasons.

In the other hemisphere, the climate may be winter, autumn, spring, or summer, and they are all changes that emerge with storms. A storm is a collision of two opposing winds and the dominant wind determines the climatic condition. In our case, as visionaries our attitude becomes the force against the other wind of life. We can rise over any storm if we can develop the right attitudes in our pursuits.

We Can Control the Winds of Time

There are some major secrets in the unfolding of time and we must understand the dynamics of them in order to achieve success through positive seeing, education, experimentations, and experiences. We have the **chronological** time, which is the accurate mathematical time and it has been arranged in a sequential disposition.

However, there are storms in this time measure and we must rise above them. For example, it may be six o'clock now and afterward seven, and progressively we come to the end of the day.

Let's take today to be Monday, so automatically the next day will be Tuesday. And if this month is January, the next month will be February. This suggests that one cannot jump from January to any other month without following the time procedure. Hence, we can rise above chronological time dictations when we learn how to harmonize and apply ourselves effectively and efficiently to work.

There's another wind of time known as *kairos*. God appoints this as a provisional, seasonal time and it could be a longer or shorter period that unfolds in our natural "sun time." We must apply ourselves to these times, which are often destined prophetic times and just a word from God in those moments can change us forever.

Thus, within a set time or times, God can pick up a gifted man on earth and show him or her His ways through revelation and use him mightily to affect and influence the world unto eternity. For instance, we are informed in Galatians 4 that "when the fullness of the time had come, God sent forth His Son" (verse 4a). Christ came to the earth and as a young supposedly unqualified Jewish rabbi, He has affected, impacted, and influenced the world more than any other person on earth.

So, one can say that *kairos* moments are the complete and perfect ordered time of God in authenticating kingdom purposes on earth via humans. And it is not for us to determine the times and seasons, which the Father has appointed unto Himself; in *kairos* moments we are obliged to wait for God's time (see Acts 1:7). This analogy supports the common adage that "God's time is the best." That's why one must be smart and discerning to know what time the calendar of our Father is and operate it by faith to achieve vision success.

However, there is another type of time that unfolds daily, noticed or unnoticed. I call that the **spirit time**. Note that a spirit or spirituality is a reality force that cannot be negated in our lives. Even humans are themselves spirit beings and we operate real life by the spirit. Spirit time is then the moment in the divine, which has no limitations and therefore, it can be superimposed over natural times. It exists as an eternal time, which has permanent eternity attached to it.

To put it in clearer language, it is important to know that spirit time has the following characteristics—the past, the present, and the future, all in the present. This is the time God lives and operates in. This can be demonstrated as is shown in the title name Alpha and Omega. God sees and lives in the end from the beginning and whatever He begins He also completes. So that as the visionary remains in God, he will likewise begin to function in the same characteristic way for his vision assignment.

We must understand that this is the best time for the people of promise. And this is also the meaning of the promise: "The LORD your God…[will] give you large and beautiful cities which you did not build, houses full of all good things, which you did not fill…vineyards and olive trees which you did not plant" (Deuteronomy 6:10-11). The spirit time is the time God delves in the past or the future times by His Spirit to get us a miracle of all times and blessings. For instance, God and the people of Israel agreed and operated in the spirit time of promise and blessing. God promises and when men obey, He blesses them.

Every promise comes with instructions and when those instructions are obeyed God releases blessings. An example where this truth was illustrated can be shown in the Bible. God instructed the people of Israel to go to the houses of their taskmasters and demand of them ornaments and as they obeyed His instructions, within 24 hours, the poor slaves became very rich and a liberated people (see Exodus 12:35-37, 50-51).

A prophetic declaration can also produce a spirit time miracle and blessing. Thus, we are admonished to believe in God so we shall be established and believe in His prophets and we prosper. Elisha said to the people of Israel that tomorrow by this time there will be food in abundance and it was so (see 2 Kings 7:1-20).

You see, one can easily say that within a space of time God can give you what others used 30 years to achieve, no matter how late it might be. Thus, if you look at your age now and the dream you have, it may take you about fifty years or more to achieve it, if you have to go by the principle of natural time.

This means that God can blow spells from the atmosphere and provide manna as it happened to the Jews in the wilderness and get you into the required fifty years immediately before the required time. This is what God meant when He said to Habakkuk that He would do a work in his day and that he would marvel when it was told: "Behold ye among the heathen, and regard, and wonder marvelously: for I will work a work in your days which ye will not believe, though it be told you" (Habakkuk 1:5 KJV).

Therefore, let's start to move in the dimension of spirit time as God's people to enable us to get what others have achieved over the years. Sometimes as a vision-oriented person, you can feel how impossible it seems for one to fulfill the promises of God in this part of the world. So one can be discouraged and start to think or use the word **can't** in his or her vocabulary. Don't ever feel pessimistic; rather, be optimistic, positive, resolute-minded, and possible oriented.

Learn how to use right dictions and avoid negative languages like "I can't" and others, which stifle the imaginations and abilities of the mind. This is because they will not encourage you; they will discourage you as the visionary. When you say, "I can't," you help constrain the mind to function creatively. We must use the interrogative form, "how can I?" and others, and this will revitalize and condition the mind to work well.

Thus, instead of saying for example, "Can we really buy lands?" let's say, "How can we buy lands?" In this case, you condition the mind to develop a summation of solutions and not compound the problem. Can we build our own schools and own chains of business enterprises? Yes, we can! Can we expand the ministries and teach our sons and daughters the wisdom of the kingdom blessing and not just the religious orders? Yes, we can! Can we raise kids who will turn into world leaders in the areas of finance, business administration, medicine, engineering? Yes, we can! Can we raise kids who will turn into world leaders as lawyers, investors, writers, activists, scholars, and important people in various disciplines of life? Yes, we CAN! I believe we will buy into the spirit times and become mighty and major forces in this region. Our children will rise up with the principle of the kingdom and influence the entire region for Jesus.

God Appoints Your Time for the Fulfillment of Every Vision in Life

This Kingdom of God is totally tied up to a revelation, which is a gift of obedience to an individual at any time. Let us read again the prophetic word in Habakkuk 2:3 (KJV): "For the vision is yet for an appointed time, but at the end it shall speak, and not lie: though it tarry, wait for it; because it will surely come, it will not tarry." What you see as a visionary is yet to come. The word "yet" means that the future blessing of the visionary is suspended in time.

So the vision-oriented person must start using the correct word— YET. For instance, if one asks the visionary, "Where is your house or wife?" he should be bold enough to give reasonable possessive and affir- mative answers to prove that he has them. Using the word yet means that the visionary believes his blessing is suspended in the future and that delays don't mean he is denied. In other words, his or her vision may be released and realized at any given time.

To Make Your Vision Plain, Write It in Simple, Understandable Language

What you see should be illustrative to people who come across the vision. In other words, vision calls for compact, concrete, explicit, and precise explanations. As a visionary, you must be able to explain your vision to the world, especially to those who will be implementing it. Explaining your vision calls for learning how to be an effective and skillful communicator impacting without ambiguity.

Rhema Williams, the author of *Everybody Can Be a Millionaire*, communicates in strong illustrative symbols and with clear examples and stories. He is of the belief that illustrative and symbolic messages stick better in people's minds and I totally agree with him. For example, we did a review on our church's anticipated growth and pattern for a year and came out with a realistic action plan.

We assumed that the entire membership of the church is five people. So we concluded that if every member invites one person each Sunday, the church would increase tremendously. We further assumed that the five members of the church can increase every week until the end of the year, with the presumption that before the end of the year the church membership will grow immensely.

You Must Communicate Your Vision Ideologically

Every true vision has a concept or ideology behind it. God gave man the power to generate ideas for wealth creation and societal influence. So every vision comes out clearly with an idea and concept.

In communicating your vision effectively, one must see to it that he clearly understands the ideology himself. Therefore, acceptable language jargons, figurative ideas, and unique positive slogans are some of the accepted means by which a visionary can effectively imprint his vision on people.

In our local church, for example, we have our own unique slogans. We have developed the ideology of preaching and training with positive statements across the board. It binds us together as visionaries. It also creates a sense of belonging and oneness. When the vision is crystal clear, it becomes easy for people to grab the concepts and occupy themselves with it in passionate moods.

Everybody knows our vision drive once he joins the church. Even our preaching is carried out with clear vision goals. Your vision is the light in your heart that illuminates your ways and this light must not be hidden. Proverbs 20:27 (KJV) states, "The spirit of man is the candle of the LORD, searching all the inward parts of the belly."

The Bible tells us that no one lights a lantern and puts it in a secret place and expects it to be seen (see Luke 11:33 KJV). We put a lantern on a table so that it dispels the darkness and grants others the opportunity to see their way. To put darkness away, one switches on the light. The vision light in you will dispel the dark circumstances around you when you force, insist, and switch it on. Many people have good dreams but because they lack a good grasp of the underlying ideology as well as the capability to communicate it well to others, their vision either lies dormant or dies.

When your vision is put in a simple, understandable, and plain language, it becomes very easy for you to consult with others when the need arises. This brings us to the issue of language. Language is very important because it is the only means to express your vision to others. Language expresses thoughts. If you cannot communicate in a simple, understandable language, your vision or ideas cannot be sold to other people.

For example, if your vision is to evangelize the country where you reside as a foreigner and you cannot communicate well in the local language, then that vision can hardly come to reality. The first step in reaching out to any set of people is to speak and communicate in their native language so that the visionary's ideologies will be understood.

A review shows that a good number of the so-called ethnic churches today have made little or no progress in winning the souls of the natives of the land for Jesus and the reason is simple: because many men of God here do not speak the local language accurately. Those who are not so fluent and perfect can't impact and influence nations. This has hindered the preaching of the gospel to people and has slowed the full integration of many foreigners into the churches.

Many of us are faced with this problem, and what do we do? Do we have to continue to live with this problem? The answer is simply no. We must communicate in the language of our hosts. So please, may I use this medium to advise all those involved to endeavor to know and understand the applicable language required in the course of preaching? We understand and share the plight of people in this part of the world due to language barriers which we cannot do much about. Yet I encourage everybody to take the bull by the horn.

Your vision requires that you invite others around the table for its accomplishment. Today, it's no longer a secret that the world has gone synergic, which shows that nothing stands alone. We can further argue that in reality everything seems to be connected with one another, so progress is achieved overwhelmingly.

Therefore, any visionary who fails to understand these facts and goes alone may face the risk of failure due to the lack of the knowledge of synergy. This can be buttressed by the popular saying, "United we stand and divided we fall."

Ordinarily, if you have the vision in the heart, it remains an individual goal, but as soon as you are able to share it with others, it helps for it to be transformed into a corporate vision. We can, therefore, define corporate vision as teamwork. That is to say, a visionary must be able to explain his dreams articulately and effectively to his audience. In reality, a vision may be personal or corporate, depending on the nature and characteristics the visionary adopts.

Personal vision is often regarded as an individual's dream, which has the characteristics of a single ideology. But a corporate vision holds the features of teamwork ideology. Teamwork is a very important element in any given vision.

When people come together to fulfill a single purpose they excellently get it done. When the visionary has been able to communicate his or her vision properly, he or she must endeavor to learn to apply the necessary language procedure, else the success of teamwork will be the downfall of the vision.

A Vision Explained Well Lays the Platform for an Activity

When you are able to communicate your vision effectively, it helps to attract others with relevant skills to come in and help translate the vision into reality. In the same way, as Christians, we must be able to convince people with noble minds in our society to accept the great challenge of kingdom building.

And to invite people, we must have the positive power of influencing and winning them to our ideological position in Christ. It is not that easy, but I believe society will embrace us when they discover that the gospel we carry has the ability to contribute meaningfully to the welfare and personal development of the people. The visionary should know that every person around him is watching with keen interest and is equally asking how he or she might be blessed or affected with the vision. Society is interested in the benefits they will get from your achievement; if not, forget it!

A well-explained vision leads to the development of others. It goes further to apposition or to complement the vision. This brings the consequence of vision expansion and growth. A vision is like a magnet. It will surely attract people of similar minds. The visionary may find some people who are passionate about his vision ideals and such people are waiting to hook up with him.

I call such people "suitable partners" and they will come along the way. Know that your vision is like a cell that picks life and soon influences growth and expansion. I consider myself privileged to have met some great people who have helped me immensely to overcome some of the challenges after several years in ministry. I believe God brought us together as like-minds in the pursuits of ministry.

Your Vision Must Have a Time Frame

Your vision will surely come to pass, it will not tarry, so wait for it. When the fullness of time comes, your vision will speak and all eyes will see. Therefore, if it seems like your vision has tarried far too long, take heart and keep preparing yourself for the day of opportunity. There's a prophetic time labeled to the vision. Your destiny time will unfold. The appointed time will manifest. That day will come. That day is an appropriate time. The vision will manifest and become a reality. The reality is futuristic, but it will surely come to pass if you don't give up.

I compare your vision to a movie that is about to be shown to the public by the filmmakers. Until the film is ready and released, nobody knows what kind of movie is being processed behind the scenes. But one day, a new sensational movie comes up on the scene that might become a sensational blockbuster film. In the same way, I can see your vision winning laurels and carrying you into the chambers of greatness and fame.

You Must Be Patient When You Have a Vision

If you cannot be patient in your vision pursuit, you may have to drop your vision and settle for something less. This is the failure of many people. They stop what they must do and initiate something else. It is often said that those who impart knowledge can equally impart error. You may be right and accurate about all that you may have taught the world without teaching them the tool of patience as a significant weapon for vision success. Again, one must note that the test of your patience is the instructive word WAIT. If one cannot wait, he likewise cannot "weight" to reach the heavyweight rank. Impatient people resent when asked to wait. The test of a person's patience is to tell him to wait. Patience is one great ingredient of vision-casting. That is why God said to Habakkuk, "Though it linger, wait for it; it will certainly come and will not delay" (Habakkuk 2:3c NIV).

VISION POINTS

1. Write your vision down.

2. Make your vision plain in an understandable and plain language.

3. Invite men for a roundtable chat on your vision.

4. When your vision remains in your heart, it is just an individual vision and not yet effective.

5. When you share your vision with the world, it becomes a corporate vision and benefits many.

6. You can achieve much in corporate vision because it is a teamwork venture.

7. Your capabilities and potentials are not determined by your skin color but by the power of your imagination.

8. Your vision speaks for you more than any advertising agency can.

9. Your vision is for an appointed time.

10. The test of your patience is the instructive word WAIT.

11. The vision which is burning in your heart is the light of life that dispels darkness and death.

WISDOM WORD

"A fulfilling visionary is an industry himself – he will not pressurize himself into desperation and therefore sell himself very cheap."

—Anonymous

Chapter 7

VISION BILLBOARDS

Every living person is born to live and fulfill a vision, which will be a contribution to the purposes of God for the world.
—Anonymous

Writing and Making the Vision Plain Motivates

The vision instruction you give others as a visionary helps people to be motivated, and it is a medium to publicize the visionary's goals. These measures can be likened to billboards to the visionary to enable him to achieve his vision. In fact, before any kind of information can appear on the billboard, colossal scales of vision successes have been registered in the books of fulfillment.

Any visionary who has been to or privileged to attend success laurels will certainly be celebrated by the entire world. We need to know who is influencing our world positively for the sake of posterity. Motivation influences and determines how far the vision will go and how it will transform people. Every visionary must motivate others in order for the dream to outlive human generations.

The efforts others make toward the accomplishment of the visionary's purpose are a total result of a visionary's command. This means that the level of activity the visionary is involved in is evidence of his vision application. The statements we put across as visionaries should be purpose-based, goal-oriented, vision-structured, and they must be able to encourage people to work diligently. No wonder King Solomon urged his subjects to be diligent (see Proverbs 12:27).

Actually, visionaries are purpose-minded and their actions culminate in the type of steps they take. So, this shows that the purpose of any type of action-step the visionary takes determines what one sees. It's believed that everybody can get what he sees when he goes for it and this includes you. And once you go for something you get it. When you go for something, endeavor to take it out rightfully or on a later date, even though you may have gone for it at the same speed as others.

Normally, the method the visionary uses to project the vision is paramount to him, which demonstrates how far he can go. The visionary is a billboard and he is meant to advertise the goals, purposes, and the benefits of this dream to the general public. In other words, he will use the medium to impact and influence the world, and his influence will be felt very soon. He automatically becomes a household name. Every step he takes as a visionary is significant to his progress and glory, and no matter how fast or slow he goes, success will be inevitable. We can learn a lesson from the potter's wheel that runs at an amazing speed but covers no distance.

The snail or the tortoise are very slow-moving creatures, yet they cover long distances over a significant period of time. One can be compared to the snail or tortoise; he will surely arrive at his vision and purpose destination no matter how slow he may be. He will eventually get there and the whole world will celebrate his arrival.

There are huge dynamic rules to every game in life and you must learn all, pertaining to your vision. One cannot ignorantly adhere to the theology and persuasive doctrine of Franz Anton Mesmer's hypnosis therapy and achieve his vision. Every living person is born to live and fulfill a vision, which will be a contribution to the purposes of God for the world. This truth cannot be denied.

Every person can get anything he works hard for and he can become the next billboard in town. The billboard status indicates where one has arrived in his career. It is a point of celebration and endorsement as a star and famous person. Nobody ever gets to the billboard stage unless he has arrived at a significant level in career skill. One must learn how to be passionate and enthusiastic for his chosen vision and purpose assignments. For example, it has been noticed by love experts that when a man is deeply in love with a woman, the man will equally requite her love for him.

Life is full of tragedies when no vision is cast. If no vision is cast, no billboard can be erected. The question is: who then will the world advertise to if there is no vision? Why can't it be you? Desire it! Work toward it! Claim it by faith! This shows and proves your vision-spirit. We need visionaries in our desires for food, clothes, books, and other services. The billboard shows the star in the making that stays tirelessly to imprint his or her vision on the hearts of men. Hence, cast and run the vision and you will be the next dream achiever on the board. For "still waters," they say, "run very deep."

As a fleeting vision, it runs high and elevates people on celebration boards for the world. Settle the vision in noble minds and let them run wild for its accomplishment. It's understandable that people are often engaged in insignificant activities when they are without a proactive vision put on board by a visionary. And as a visionary, one should be proactive and not reactive to circumstances. No external issues will compromise your persuasive ideas to act abruptly. The vision-driven person should act based on an inner-driven and persuasive mind.

Vision Is the Antidote for Greatness

The positive consequences of an explained vision are an antidote for greatness. Do you have a vision? Then be bold and courageous to explain it to the world. The bold and courageous explanation one gives of his vision is important to one's vision success and how far one's name will go. Success in vision equally makes fame, greatness, and honor.

Ordinarily, a common person can become popular and famous due to his bold declarations and projective convocations, which lead to an extraordinary achievement. It's on record that men follow visions systemically when they are well explained. And they equally get to their desired glory and fame when they stay on course. So explain yourself well and pursue your life's career with good intentions and abilities.

We can relate this same idea to Winston Churchill who saw economic instability and potential crisis in the entire world if Adolf Hitler's threats were not checked. He was bold enough to explain courageously to the then leaders and people of the world about the inherent dangers. And up till date, he has been remembered by this notable achievement, which has become one of his major vision assignments as Prime Minister of Britain. Today, the world is saved because of his vision for world peace.

And today's leaders draw inspiration from him and therefore, they are equally motivated to halt any negative action by any world leader to disturb world peace. In the same vein, the famous "I have a dream" speech of the social and political activist Martin Luther King Jr. against racism in America changed the perception of the entire American people toward people of color. What about Martin Luther, the reformist, whose vision was to transform the religious beliefs of his time to conform to the Word of faith?

A popular world leader from South Africa, Nelson Mandela, explained to the then apartheid regime the need for equal rights and freedom for both whites and blacks. He was a living legend, a testimony of fame and achievement. The crown of his vision success is seen in his transformation from the prison courtyard to the presidential palace. The world witnessed the honor bestowed on him when he received the Nobel Peace Prize, among others.

Also, Conrad Hilton explained himself well about his intentions to build a chain of first-class hotels. He achieved his dream before his death. By the time he died, he had already built over 75 hotels in America alone, plus many more in Europe. Henry Ford also explained the bold vision to make cars a necessity product instead of being luxurious and ostentatious products. His dream was realized. Today, Ford cars are everywhere and they are only comparable to none.

The Gillette mogul, King Gillette, also thought and produced the popular razor blade that we use in beautifying and shaping the human looks. We can name as many visionaries as possible: Jeff Bezos, the world's richest man, Walt Disney of Disney World, John Cohen of Tesco supermarkets, and Harland Sanders of Kentucky Fried Chicken. There is also a Sir Richard Branson of Virgin Group limited companies, and Silvio Berlusconi, former Prime Minister of Italy, who is a successful businessman and renowned politician. Others are Tiger Woods, the golf icon, Michael Jackson, the pop star legend, Michael Jordan, the dream angel of basketball and a proprietor of a renowned basketball team—the Charlotte Hornets. The aforementioned names are of world leaders who understood and believed in the values of positive vision. They discovered, celebrated, and shared their personal visions to the people of the world and today they are all billboards in their respective disciplines and assignments. You too can become one of them if you won't relent and stagnate along the way of your vision pursuit and if you will take time to understand the values of the power of positive seeing.

It is important for you to remember that if you cannot explain yourself boldly and courageously, you cannot accomplish your dreams anywhere in this world. So, it's paramount to explain your vision appropriately. There are some basic areas one has to explain periodically when a vision is cast. All the people involved in a synergic project must have a good grasp of their respective assignments as the visionary communicates the entire vision.

For instance, if one's family is involved in the team, then it's of great importance that they must know the "key points" or the "engine" that moves the vision. In this context, may I use this medium to ask some questions about your vision? Is anybody aware of the direction you are moving now as a visionary? Do these people know the target and dream of the vision for the year? The power of positive vision has no limitation whether you are a church leader or otherwise. You should endeavor to show the required road map for the year.

We cannot just think that we are led by the Spirit so the Spirit will lead us in our endeavors. In the real sense, the Spirit that leads us does so by the element of our minds and hearts.

One must know that the world is a place of vision-casting and vision-execution. Every day we see people going about their duties because they all have their respective dreams, visions, and goals, which spell out their purposes.

The truth is that you cannot run in life without a vision and if you do so, you can become a fool. It's believed that it's the unwise who runs without definite knowledge and specific direction. This aspect of vision fulfillment is very essential. Let us relate this analogy to myself; I like to use my local church in giving example because we have a specific vision with definite assignments and goals. One can also relate this to his or herself.

The ICGC-Driven Vision

The International Central Gospel Church (ICGC) has a vision. Our vision is to establish the house of God through the development of model New Testament Christians and churches. The source of the vision started in one man, Dr. Mensa Otabil, but the purpose of the vision had its engagement and operation in many more others in the world.

God has given us a specific and definite kind of revelation relevant for human progress and spiritual development and frequently seen, the greatest corporation is when men build another man's vision for them to fulfill their own visions. Wherever we go, we are guided to shape vision, raise leaders, and influence society through Christ. This has been the means by which we have obtained our vision and realized its impact in the world. We are faith gospel preachers and through our recipe of vision and mission we have influenced many people in the world. We are a church with a vision and if any individual joins us, he is obliged to have a deep sense of a definite vision to live. We help shape people's vision in the will, intent, and purpose of God for their lives. Anytime we are privileged to have a guest that may have a distorted vision, we help such a person to see things in the direction of a purpose-driven life.

We equally help people to discover their visions if they have not realized them. It's amazing to know that some people see no need to have a vision. It seems to me that many people are living a distorted life so that they can hardly be upright. It's clear that how one thinks is how one walks and lives, just as the popular adage goes, "the way you make your bed is the way you lie on it."

I, therefore, presume that it is not just joining ICGC or otherwise, and just to be a nominal member; instead, one should endeavor to have his goals and aspirations. God has called people together to contribute their various talents and gifts to further His Kingdom and I believe everybody knows this. I am persuaded to believe that every single face one sees in our church or in the world is a gift and a relevant player to the realization and actualization of great things on the earth realm.

Hence, as members of the body of Christ, we must be fully prepared to contribute our quota to God's work everywhere under the vision-umbrella we operate in. As future leaders, we must be able to lead everyone into his or her gifts and abilities through the guiding principle of one's vision statement. We must push each one to his respective area and assignment God has destined. So, let's arise and shine, for the time has come and the glory of the Lord is at hand.

The Mensa Otabil-Driven Vision

The General Overseer and Senior Pastor, Dr. Mensa Otabil, is noted for his strong beliefs in his vision assignment and purpose. He preaches the gospel of Christ with a specific vision in order to uplift the image of mankind, particularly the black man, and address solutions to our pertinent problems. Through his messages, he has given hope to the hopeless and also raised leaders in different aspects of life. Through his efforts, many ordinary people have become more proactive in society. His vision is absolutely specific and definite, and I am a product of his ministry.

The point is clear—God rules in the affairs of men and one should not limit the gifts of God. I agree to the fact that a functional man is always a gift through whom the world can be blessed. Let's be functional people from now onward like Queen Esther. We are born for such a time as this and if we perish with our vision, we perish unto the glory of the Father who is the source of all positive visions and human purposes. May we become vision-oriented as members of the body of Christ.

The African Vision Pathology

It's eminent that because of the selfishness of some of our forefathers and previous leaders on our continent, we are lagging behind in progress. Quite recently, one institution came out with a report that Africa is backward over two hundred years in relation to the United States of America. How absurd! However, self-centered attitudes and beliefs of most of the African people may be one of our major heritage pathologies.

It is pathetic when one hears on radio and television painful remarks stating that "Africa has no hope of catching up with ill governance and a lack of vision." Or that "lack of vision turns investors away from the African continent." Or that "most of the hot zone conflicts are in Africa." Or that "Africans' share of global production is one percent." Or that "there are very few success stories in the African continent." Or that "oil in Nigeria is a curse due to inequality and religious conflicts and oil-rich regions in Sudan are torn apart." Or that "brain drain is a major problem of Africa." (Aljazeera News 11-07-2008)

We may have inherited liabilities instead of true legacies. It is quite clear that backwardness is evidence of lack of vision and nothing else, but our passion for change can produce a new breed of people who will possess the earth and share their blessing with the entire world. Therefore, the pathological disease of the African is his distorted selfish vision, which ends in lack of vision and sightlessness. But he can change it now.

I have never considered the fundamental African crisis as a leadership problem. It's due to lack of vision. This has gone a long way to delay the African people in every aspect of life. The real pathological ill of Africa is idolatry, which has degenerated and degraded the richest land on earth to produce the poorest people. It's a problem of idolatry and we must look into it for reversal.

When we go into the ancient historical records, it stands out clearly as a fact that the source of idolatry is from Africans. Africans initiated idolatry and they have expanded its tentacles into the entire world through the slave trade and relocations from Africa to the other parts of the world. It is also a fact that most Africans keep and maintain idolatry as a cultural practice, which in no small measure has helped ruin Africa. This unhealthy practice can be noticed from the rank and file of African people.

I always preach that idolatry is the greatest sin against God in the entire world and the highest moral disgrace on earth as well. (This may be limited to my point of view.) If you go into idol worship, you attract the wrath of God, though all other disobedience is disobedience. Read Hebrews 11 and read about the heroes of faith; you will notice that the records are without three great kingdom generals. The author made a roll call from the beginning to his time and three major godly players were missing—Aaron, Saul, and Solomon.

Aaron was the first high priest, Saul was the first king of Israel, and Solomon was the first wise king on earth. But we don't see their names among the heroes of faith in Hebrews 11, although God made mention of some of them in the New Testament. The author of the book of Hebrews mentions Aaron severally in his book but failed to recognize him in chapter 11. I discovered to my amazement that these great Bible personalities practiced idolatry and hence, their names were not included in Hebrews 11.

In this way, we can learn a good lesson and change from our cultural and ancient practices and get transformed through the renewal of our minds (see Romans 12:2). We must get transformed from our ancient ills and be transformed to the Word of God. This is the only remedy for us if we want to see progress in our vision missions in Africa.

The Logic of Wealth and Riches

Wealth creation and riches are not bound by any specific rules per se. Rather, it's strongly an internally discovered virtue. As visionaries, we should endeavor to look within ourselves and generate the required wealth and riches for humanity. We must look within ourselves and generate enormous wealth and riches via our potentials, gifts, and talents. We must build our lives and nations from within ourselves to fulfill our purpose-driven visions. We should equally generate positive ideas and right principles through our own people to make wealth and riches.

This means that as vision-oriented explorers, we cannot uphold the verdicts of any selfish leader and continue to migrate to other lands to suffer and perish without considering the rich deposits in our lives that breed overwhelming wealth. And if we look around ourselves, it looks as if we are going forward very slowly and sometimes we stand still for years.

Any act of man without a release of his potential, gift, and talent, generates stress, difficulties, enslavements, and ultimately poverty. It's known that nothing precedes one's potential, gift, and talent. The up and down movement of people must never be as a result of a set circumstance against them, but as a motive for purpose fulfillment, interrelational purposes, the wisdom of exploration and tourism, among others.

We must improve ourselves with the talents God has given to us by working hard and depending on Him. Men who tap in the reservoir of talents and gifts get richer and wealthier more than others who seem to be jobbing around. In so doing, we will become self-determinant, self-respected, and self-valued. I, therefore, implore every individual to endeavor to search inward in the pursuit of wealth and riches.

Definite Knowledge Is Power

There is a common and accepted adage that states that "knowledge is power." How false this seems and how effective it is as a deceit. Thinking that getting knowledge is enough for success in life could be a plot against human progress. Specific and definite knowledge is power and not just knowledge per se. People have knowledge, yet it could be ignorance and such ignorance can never be said to have power, except for the destruction of the person.

I believe that he who has definite and positive knowledge has power. The knowledge that empowers people and gives them advantage over the rest of the people is always definite and specialized. Remember, God always empowers whomsoever He calls and assigns him or her with definite vision knowledge that triggers advantages for men.

Therefore, wherever we may find ourselves in search for the so-called greener pastures, the various systems on the new terrain shall not be in our favor if we lack the required gut, skill, and acumen. Any person, irrespective of where he finds himself, requires definite and specific knowledge or greater power to be able to fulfill his purpose. Even if one finds himself at any location with abundant milk and honey, he must equally be able to avail himself with the specific resource that abounds.

We cannot achieve our personal vision and dreams on a battlefield we have no definite knowledge about, unless the God of Heaven guides our tour. It does greater harm than good if you see what you want yet may not know how to get it.

Our comrades are in prison, sidelined, marginalized, and relegated to the dungeon of isolation because they misunderstand the pattern by which the game of success and wealth creation is executed. Some have died prematurely, some are struggling apathetically with the defeat attitude of "give up and throw in the towel for the center can no longer hold; everything has fallen apart." Whenever or wherever people possess specific technical knowledge they easily breakthrough and succeed. You too can breakthrough if you apply definite and specific knowledge in all your endeavors.

Thinking Breeds Definite Knowledge

How can one achieve the power of good thought? The answer is one must take time out to think. You must endeavor to think positively and when you do you will acquire reasonable and specific knowledge, which can equally help you to acquire wealth and riches. This book has a specific way it imparts knowledge. It's centered on the principles of self-philosophy and the art of positive thinking on vision. It is a product of research, personal efforts, and strong desires.

Note that the Bible says that as a man thinks in his heart so is he (see Proverbs 23:7a). This means one cannot rise above his own thinking and he is a total summation of his own thoughts. One's own thoughts and lines of thinking are what one sows and reaps. Think and grow well and live longer on earth! Thinking right breeds insurmountable success and wealth creation. It's believed that one's facial expression is a total reflection of the way he thinks. Your own thinking is your true identity and composure, which projects you to the world.

Have you ever allotted some time to consider and re-consider who you are and why? The billboard is waiting for people who think rightly for the achievement of specific and definite goals on earth. You are born to be somebody and the only way to know that is through the art of thinking. We master life by thinking. Every single person has a billboard to display. You should be somewhere, not everywhere.

You are positioned to play a part in the game of life, so find it and do just that. Do you have a clue about God's mind for your life? (See Jeremiah 29:11.) What does God want you to think about? I believe it's His Word through which you can discover and develop your vision and purpose from. What about the vision God has for you? Have you sought out His mind for your life? The Bible contains specific words for you alone and they come through revelations. This makes the Bible timely, up-to-date, and unchangeable.

Run Your Own Vision

Running your vision is essential because your vision speaks for you more than anyone else. You definitely attract success by the person you become through your own steering vision. "Every man is born successful," says Helen Keller. But future success depends on what you do presently. People will see your activity and say, "Truly, this man or woman has a fulfilling vision."

No wonder the Bible says that we would know them by their fruits (see Matthew 7:16a).

When one displays a good and right habit, others will be willing to emulate him in everything. You can easily assist others and they will accept it without arguments when they see you as a man or woman of accomplishment. When you are running any vision, you must know that those who run in a race receive a price. So run so that you may equally obtain the crown (see 1 Corinthians 9:24-25). For us Christians, we run with the vision of God to obtain an incorruptible crown of the Kingdom.

Stop being egocentric because it's a reactive vice that can hold back your confidence and all your abilities. Cease from leaning on your own understanding because you will fail and this will amount to disgrace, and where there's no grace, disgrace is imminent and inevitable. Egocentric self-dependent folks can easily develop that erroneous thought that there's a hidden enemy working against them, no matter how hard they try. I advise that since each one of us has a vision, purpose, and specific assignments as smaller parts of the bigger picture of life, we must be able to develop our own visions for easy assessment.

You Can Be the Next Celebrated King

A celebrated king is an individual who has worked so hard on his personal vision he has learned how to assess the future with the mind-set of a winner who depends on God. Such an individual is blessed with the ability to think and understand logical methods that conquer and bring trophies. He is easily considered as the next celebrity and live wire of the vision in the boardroom. Anybody who is privileged to be in the boardroom can become a billboard himself for others to emulate. They rise and go to the acclaimed top as heroes, not stars.

In our modern generation, one can do any negative vice and rise to stardom and fame. People of today get involved in negative practices and rise to the top the next morning through the power of the paparazzi. This kind of rise to stardom is detrimental to us as human beings.

I believe that the heroes we must adore are those who have selflessly applied their lives and efforts to specific purposes that bring overwhelming progress to humanity. They achieve and persistently work hard in a chosen humanity effort and development and offer systematic solutions to our problems, and so they rise to the top of fame. These heroes must be on the billboard as our adored icons.

Vision Is the Key That Unlocks World Treasures

Societies want assistance from men and women of vision irrespective of their race and geographical location. So do not say, "Because I am a foreigner in the location where I find myself, I cannot offer anything apart from what the citizens want me to do."

The visionary has created a rich encyclopedia and when I consulted it for knowledge the phrase, "I am a foreigner," was never found. If your vision is good and well placed, you can demonstrate it anywhere and people will be proud to be part of it. The Heavens then become one's limit and the reward remains forever.

For example, two great men of God from Nigeria, Matthew Ashimolowo and Sunday Adelaja, have proven in Europe that the kingdom concept of living is not limited to an individual or a geographical environment and human philosophy. And wherever one works the Word of God, the Word will work for him too. You can establish God's kingdom model anywhere God calls and assigns in order to replace every demonic system on earth.

These two men of God have established megachurches as missionaries in both the Eastern and Western blocs in Europe. You too can be the next kingdom authority in your chosen career and the billboard in your neighborhood, nation, and even worldwide to display your glory.

Vision Has a Reward

Every vision on earth has a reward. The reward of your vision is the payoff day where your check will be issued to be cashed. The glory of your vision is the success of fulfillment it creates as evidential deeds in the public eyes. When the vision begins to contribute to the development of mankind and society, it has succeeded in its orientation.

As can be noted in this book, we know vividly that every vision that is carried out well has a reward. This is revealed in the Bible when Peter asked Jesus what would be the disciples' reward seeing they had left everything to follow Him and His ministry (see Matthew 19:27). Jesus replied that there is no one who leaves his father and mother, brothers and sisters, properties and every material thing and follows Him, who will not receive back on this earth a hundredfold and afterward be given eternal life in the Kingdom of God (see Matthew 19:29).

As we know, reward is different from a gift. Gift is given based on love and not labor. But when we talk about reward, it is based on what we have done and therefore we merit it. Gift then is not given based on merit. Rewards are and they come at the end of labor. We can't expect a gift; we must expect our reward when we have undertaken a labor. So then, if one works he expects his wages or salary at the end. This is because reward is given after labor and not as a gift. As Apostle Paul encouraged the church of Corinth, "Therefore, my beloved brethren, be ye steadfast, unmoveable, always abounding in the work of the Lord, forasmuch as ye know that your labour is not in vain in the Lord" (1 Corinthians 15:58 KJV).

The purpose of the reward in vision declaration and accomplishment is for the Christian to live a better life on earth. For this reason, one must carry out his vision according to the will of God: because God will see to his reward.

VISION POINTS

1. Our talents contribute to further our vision fulfillments.

2. Don't let anyone tell you who you are and what you can do.

3. You need to discover yourself to break limitation off your vision.

4. Given opportunity, you can perform like any other person on earth.

5. The Holy Spirit is your divine enablement to fulfilling your vision to the ultimate.

6. There is a reward for your vision.

7. Procrastination and complacency impede the progress of our vision.

8. Non-adherence to vision principles can be an obstacle in vision pursuit.

9. Don't lean on your own understanding.

10. You can be the next celebrity on the billboards.

11. For vision breakthrough, you must think and arrive at specific and definite knowledge.

12. Each terrain requires some special knowledge about the environment and how one can function in it.

WISDOM WORD

"You must have long-range goals to keep you from being frustrated by short-range failures."

—Charles C. Nobel

Chapter 8

THE CHURCH REPRESENTS GOD'S VISION

When Jesus came into the coasts of Caesarea Philippi, he asked his disciples, saying, Whom do men say that I the Son of man am? And they said, Some say that thou art John the Baptist: some, Elias; and others, Jeremias, or one of the prophets. He saith unto them, But whom say ye that I am? And Simon Peter answered and said, Thou art the Christ, the Son of the living God. And Jesus answered and said unto him, Blessed art thou, Simon Barjona: for flesh and blood hath not revealed it unto thee, but my Father which is in heaven. And I say also unto thee, That thou art Peter, and upon this rock I will build my church; and the gates of hell shall not prevail against it. And I will give unto thee the keys of the kingdom of heaven: and whatsoever thou shalt bind on earth shall be bound in heaven: and whatsoever thou shalt loose on earth shall be loosed in heaven. Then charged he his disciples that they should tell no man that he was Jesus the Christ.

—Matthew 16:13-20 KJV

The Church Is Christ's Embassy on Earth

The church's embassy is God's vision and institution for the Kingdom of Heaven on earth. The church is an embassy for Heaven and no one can ever enter Heaven without it. For instance, any person who will want to visit the United States of America or any other country for that matter, should go to its embassy in his or her country and obtain the necessary and required documentation; other than that, one must forget it or be a fugitive who will be repatriated when caught in that country. This is because that territory in your own country has legal and sovereign powers. It is also considered as foreign country in your own country by international law.

In the same vein, the church is a territorial land of Heaven on earth and we need to be weaned through salvation before we can ever enter Heaven. And it is founded and built on the foundation of Jesus Christ alone. So then, we humans receive the spirit of revelation from the Father after accepting and accessing this unparalleled truth.

We henceforth become partakers of God's divine nature and escape the corruption and lust in this world (see 2 Peter 1:4). It's revealing, as Jesus pointed out, that one's ability to know and discover the divine nature of Jesus as the Christ elevates the individual to a spiritual dimension of blessing. Many people in this world cannot accept this truth and this has given rise to many religions on earth. It's vital to also know that no amount of civilized knowledge, research studies, and religious wisdom in the material world can produce the degree of elevation that comes as a result of kingdom revelation.

And from the above passage, it amounts to the fact that a revelation can be given to a man when a question is asked. A good question then reveals the mental level of a person and how one should be sought for, for help or be helped. Jesus then asked His disciples a very good inescapable question regarding His person, which was crucial for their development and elevation.

Mostly, people including His own disciples saw Him as just one of the anointed servants of God. This is because they looked at Him and saw Him under the paradigm of human thoughts, which is often based mainly on public opinion: some say that You are John the Baptist, others say, You are Elijah or Jeremiah; or one of the great prophets.

Then Christ limited the big circle and confined it to their personal opinion about His true identity and person. After all, they had been around him for quite some time now. It was this kind of test that revealed the dimension of thought some of them had reached. Peter came out boldly among the 12 and said, "You are the Christ, the Son of the living God" (Matthew 16:16). Jesus then released the secret ambassadorial kingdom vision and model called *ecclesia* or "called out ones," or the "sanctified and set apart," "the church," and its purpose of establishment.

The Church Reveals the Will, Intent, and Purpose of God on Earth

The church established by Christ reveals the will, intent, and purpose assignment of God on earth and it also influences men as to what must be done on earth. What is the will of God? My primary school teacher once taught that God's will is the reign of the will of God in the hearts of men. How profound this definition is!

This equally reveals that when the Father manifests kingdom wisdom to any of His disciples, a kingdom vision and goal through His will, intent, and purpose can immediately be established on earth. And with the establishment of such kingdom virtues on earth, kingdom keys can also be released to him who can then determine what must be done both in Heaven and on earth. The fact goes that the key you hold will determine the gate you can open.

Let us also make this logical analogy using countries and their embassies. For example, what America or any other country does in diplomatic circles depends on the type of reports that overseas embassies send to the home country. This will determine, influence, and portray the ideas and intentions of the country over the other.

What the overseas embassies say is what the home country accepts and endorses. This is what Christ meant when He said, "And whatever you bind on earth will be bound in heaven, and whatever you loose on earth will be loosed in heaven" (Matthew 16:19b-c). Wow! We send information about the earth realm and we in turn tell what Heaven must do here.

It's crucial to know that the "human antenna" that positions itself well catches Heaven's frequencies in revelations and visions and this act helps to release kingdom keys. These keys are the resources we need because they help us to take dominion authority and power over creation. One must equally come to terms with the fact that flesh and blood can never ever be in a position to catch kingdom revelations. This is revealed as the other disciples relied on human opinions and therefore, deviated from Heaven's vision.

It's also revealing that anytime we allow God to show us something, He equally takes up the task to build what He reveals to us. In Matthew 16:18b Jesus said, "I will build My church," and not "you will build My church." We humans are only powerful tools and entrustments in the hands of the Master Builder. This is the understanding King David had about the work of God when he wrote in Psalms 127:1 (KJV), "Except the LORD build the house, they labour in vain that build it: except the LORD keep the city, the watchman waketh but in vain."

It is evident that what God builds on the earth realm is immune against the invasions and attacks of Satan. The gates of the kingdom of Hell cannot stand against the church when we stay focused and attuned. Hell can only stand and prevail over what man builds, which is outside God's will, intent, and purpose on earth or otherwise, when we become negligent and complacent.

We Are Diplomats and Ambassadors In God's Kingdom

The church is the embassy and vision of God and the employers in the church are the ambassadors of Christ. Apostle Paul admonishes in 2 Corinthians 5:20 (KJV) and it is worth considering here: "Now then we are **ambassadors for Christ**, as though God did beseech you by us: we pray you in Christ's stead, be ye reconciled to God."

This verse of Scripture vindicates and positions believers as the ambassadors sent from the Kingdom of Heaven. As diplomats, we are protected and covered. And as the medium by which Heaven relates to the earth, every resource needed has been provided for. We are on the priority list in Heaven and immediately we send signals; resources of all kinds are sent immediately to us on earth.

The church is also a "seeker place" where all humans (should) come and be transformed, restored, and justified to be partakers of God's divine family, both in Heaven and on earth (see Ephesians 1:10). When we respond to these graceful blessings, we are labeled as believers "in Christ." A believer is simply a person who has accepted the redemptive work of Christ over his life. An unbeliever is a person who has refused to accept the redemptive work of God through Jesus Christ.

There are two types of sins. We have the Adamic sin, which is through the heritage of our humanity; and we have personal sin, which is our self-inflicted weakness to live obediently and righteously as dominion agents on earth. Hence, we must note this in particular, for us Christians there's no more Adamic sin issue here; but for unbelievers, both Adamic and personal sin stand. As humans in general, we have just one sin hanging on our necks, and this sin is the sin of refusal of Christ Jesus as Lord and Savior. And regarding personal sins for us Christians, the Apostle John states that "if we confess our sins, He is faithful and just to forgive us our sins and to cleanse us from all unrighteousness" (1 John 1:9).

After the death and resurrection of Christ, Adamic sin is annulled for us who have believed into Him. Christ has wiped away our sins with His precious blood. The sin of refusing Jesus as Christ and Savior is the only sin left which Christ can't use His blood to wipe away. We use our personal decisions to put this yoke on our necks. This is the only sin that has enslaved people and likely to lead them toward Hell and no religious rituals can provide a remedy.

The precious blood of Christ Jesus, the Lamb, has paid for any other type of sin. Those who refuse the gift offer of God remain disobedient and unbelievers and they can never ever run their God-given visions and purposes on earth. These people can never ever wash their sins away and they may remain perpetual sinners who will not be "wives" of Christ. We accept Jesus as our Lord and Savior and as our precious husband whose responsibility is to wash us. We come to Him with filth and He cleanses us up to use us for the kingdom vision.

The Church Is the Divine "Wife" of Christ

The church is the divine wife of Christ (see Ephesians 5:25-32). And anytime we talk about marriage, we must endeavor never to separate the husband from the wife because they are one in the sacrament of matrimony. They are obliged to run their purposes, visions, and lives in union as one flesh. Some people on earth have requited the love of Christ and by this impressive act they are transformed and espoused to Christ. For this He made sure that His potential spouse supports and accentuates the vision and purpose, which is committed to Him on earth; and the sacrament of matrimony guarantees support of a man's dream more than any other type of relationship.

The mystery of oneness with Christ through spiritual wedlock gives us the power and authority to uphold, defend, and run a common kingdom vision and purpose in life. This act equally consolidates and perpetuates the kingdom vision and purpose for creation. And it is through righteousness, elevation, mercy, prosperity, protection, and security that Heaven supports the earth realm.

So I believe that when we talk about the church and Christ, we are dealing with a sensitive, spiritual mystery only the Spirit of God can help us understand. Christ has a hearty "divine wife" and He approaches her plainly in all things that pertain to life and godliness. We are inseparable and closely knitted together in harmony because He's the Head.

It's revealed that for two persons to come together to become "one," the following five important ingredients should be present to form automatic action steps to be able to fulfill the vision, will, intent, and purpose of the Father:

1. There is always disassociation and reunion from one's original family to a new one. It has always been likened to the way and manner Christ left the Father in Heaven and cleaved to us on earth so that we could become one flesh (see Ephesians 5:30-31 KJV).

2. It automatically introduces a new head of a family, as also Christ is the Head and we are the body, which has been interwoven

together to demonstrate the full picture of the developed image and the church structure. This is the real model of kingdom vision God wants to establish on earth (see Ephesians 5:23).

3. It's an everlasting and eternal union, which must be respected with total obedience in accordance with the principles and cannot be disannulled or terminated in divorce. God said, "I will never leave you nor forsake you" (Hebrews 13:5c; cf. Deuteronomy 31:6c; Joshua 1:5c).

4. It is the foundation for the establishment and stability of love for one another. Christ loves us with perfect love (see Ephesians 5:25). He has totally given Himself to us so that He can wash us pure and holy from our filth and rudiments of sin, and present us to Himself—glorious, spotless, without blemishes, and wrinkles (see Ephesians 5:25-27).

5. It introduces the promise of humility and loyalty to each other. In our case as the church, oily-fragranced prayer is poured out toward Heaven to Christ, "our Head," who is seated at the right hand of the Father and He responds with answers that flow to the lower parts of His body (the church) and that is where we draw our anointing and grace for nourishment.

This is most probably the reason why Jesus warned us not to lose our salt or light in the world. As divine "wives," we must passionately share the ideals of Christ's vision without division. The church is supposed to be the salt of preservation and the light of enlightenment, illumination, and vision.

The Holy Spirit Is the Live Wire between Heaven and Earth

The Spirit of God is the live wire, link, coordinating element, and connection between earth and Heaven; and this is actualized through the existence of the church and its God-given vision. Without the active presence of the Holy Ghost, no man can initiate, cultivate, enhance, and activate kingdom visions and missions on earth. And God preserves the earth and its inhabitants or resources through the active presence of the Holy Ghost in the church.

In the same way, when the Holy Ghost and the church are absent from the earth, destruction will be inevitable. I know that one day this will be the condition of the world and it will be catastrophic and disastrous. It has long been prophesied that one day the earth will fall flat, and nothing good will ever be experienced because the Holy Spirit and the church (which preserves and conserves the earth) shall be taken away. Everything abounds now because of the omnipresent Holy Spirit and the body of Christ.

The earth is preserved now because God's good news and presence of life are still here. Jesus announced to His disciples about His future departure. But Jesus's answer to them revealed a secret. It was as if He had said that they shouldn't weep anymore because He would be with them always even to the end (see Matthew 28:20b). What He meant by saying that He would be with them and in them, was that His body (the church) would remain on earth while His head would be with the Father (see John 14:17c).

Christ Jesus is still here in His body and His authority at the right hand side of the Father is advocating for us in Heaven. The Holy Spirit repositioning is a coordinated live wire effort to preserve the church and transform the earth through the vision of God.

The State/Consequences of Fallen Man

The emergence of bad satanic news resulted through human failure and the advancement of wicked activities on earth. Man got dethroned from his original dominion authority where God placed him and he became enslaved to sin and disobedience. Self-depravation, purpose abuses and lack of purpose, impaired vision and lack of vision, wickedness, and pride became the conditions and circumstances man found himself with.

The bait that destroyed man is the bad news Satan still employs after many generations. Satan tilts the truth to suit his lies and we fall victims all the time. We must, therefore, be vigilant because our enemy roars like a lion to devour us (see 1 Peter 5:8). The disobedience and fall of humanity was a direct result of our developed faith in his bad news and doubts in the good news God has already made available.

We all know that what one hears eventually determines what one believes and becomes (see Romans 10:17). We are influenced to have faith or doubt based on the kind of information that gets into our hearts and minds. And the evil things we believe position us to be accusers and rebellious. This is why it is important to guard and protect our ears, and also we must be able to manage the information that comes to us.

The evil news of Satan generates wrong faith and leads us to fail in kingdom visions and purposes. Man was separated from the sovereign kingdom and has become an outcast galloping away—visionless and sightless. As a result of all these set of circumstances, the devil then controls our world and abuses both humanity and creation.

The Emergence of Christ and Its Significance

Jesus Christ came on earth as a deliverer and restorer. Christ's possible mission introduced a powerful counteractive blessing, which destroys satanic bad news and its attendant effects (see John 1:3-8). It should be worthy of note that Christ Jesus came to do three major things among others for mankind on earth.

1. He came to restore, reintroduce, and reestablish the lost kingdom of humanity.

2. He also came to reintroduce, reestablish, and restore Heaven back to the earth realm as one major component of rulership in the universe domain via connectivity with the Holy Spirit.

3. He came to fix humans back to their original source of existence for absolute survival and dominion life.

Consequently, through this benevolent act, we have been able to tap back into both our divine and our natural sources of creation for our potential, purpose, and vision to function perfectly in all things. The greatest mystery and controversy is that God manifested as a person to destroy the works of the enemy. I believe that every single work of Satan is destroyed through Christ's birth, ministry, death, resurrection, and ascension from the earth realm to the position of advocacy in Heaven (see John 1:1, 14; 1 Timothy 3:16; 1 John 3:8b).

The greatest destruction and devastation Christ had over Satan was obtained by the shedding of His blood for our disobedience, the message of reconciliation He preached for restoration, His death and invasion of Hades, and the recovering of the keys of man's dominion authority back to man. Thus, the total embodiment of all the activities of Jesus Christ is what is termed as salvation. Romans 8:37a (KJV) says, "Nay, in all these things we are more than conquerors."

Salvation Reinstates Us to a Position of Kingdom Vision

The purpose of salvation is to reinstate humans back to where they were before the fall. Salvation is a medium through which man can reach out to God's Kingdom. In this context, it can be said to be the means of transport to the end of our purpose destination and not an end in itself as our purpose orientation.

This is crucial to understand. The purpose of Christ's death and resurrection was to make His mission on earth a possible achievable expedition. He needed to die in order to make salvation an issue of reality to all mankind and in order to reinstate us to the position of seeing positively into Heaven's kingdom visions.

Hence, salvation becomes the vehicle that transports us into our designated, destined purposes and not as the purpose itself. Salvation can be termed as a halfway picture necessary for the whole dominion picture. We should herewith consider salvation as a halfway house and not a full house in itself. We may live short of our lives and purposes when we settle on salvation as the reason why Christ came to the earth.

Instead, we must inherit salvation as the true medium through which we become partakers of God's divine nature and are then able to be the proper dominion agents. Salvation is therefore presumed to be a pointer to a place of purpose and dominion and not vice versa.

As we consider the aforementioned, it can then be argued that salvation is not the primary preoccupation of God; it has become His strategic plan through which His most preoccupied intentions manifest. For God to reach His utmost intentions and goals, salvation is used as a key weapon for breakthroughs. And how vital it is as salvation cannot be changed or be replaced. Salvation has become a sensitive, significant preoccupation issue without which God can't restore, reestablish, and reintroduce humans as the perfect authorities on earth.

This also means that we don't become saved to be qualified candidates for Heaven alone; rather, we become saved so that we can apply Genesis 1:28 on the earth once again. Although it can be assumed that we can go to Heaven as spiritual beings to have communion with the family above, we become saved and restored to our proper positions as better rulers, fit as authorities, domain controllers, and people of influence on the earth realm. This is the original intention of God for every person. This is the reason why Jesus came to the earth—He came to fulfill all righteousness and open the floodgates of Heaven once more for us.

Dominion Is the Original Intention of God for Man

The original intention of God for mankind on earth is found in Genesis 1:28 (KJV): "And God blessed them, and God said unto them, Be fruitful, and multiply, and replenish the earth, and subdue it: and have dominion over the fish of the sea, and over the fowl of the air, and over every living thing that moveth upon the earth." Here we see that God gave mankind power over the skies, lands, and waters. Through the power of vision, we have divine authority over natural and spiritual entities in the domains above.

Genesis Chapter Three Has No Place in the Mind of God

Dr. Myles Monroe has stated in several of his books the fact that the first three chapters of Genesis explain it all for man. He said that it is believed that Genesis chapter one is a verbal narrative chapter because God spoke creation into existence. Chapter two is an explanation and actualization chapter because it shows when God put His hand on work to start creation. And chapter three is an interruption and distraction chapter because it highlighted the activity of Satan in creation. And the rest of the Scriptures are restorative chapters of the Bible because they demonstrate all the endeavors of God to bring us back to Genesis chapters one and two.

It has therefore been argued by some Bible scholars that Genesis chapter three has no perfect place in the original program intended by Heaven or God. The question then is, if it is not part of the original plan of God, then chapter three should not have existed at all. If Satan had not interrupted there would be no need for man to seek salvation.

Salvation May Probably Be Considered as Genesis Chapter Three

So, we may go further to discuss that salvation should replace Genesis chapter three and that will send us back to Genesis chapter two whereby we'll assume our original occupational assignment of dressing and keeping the earth (see Genesis 2:15). We cultivate, decorate, design, beautify, and polish the earth in absolute maintenance as lords of the earth. And when we do this perfectly, we can say without an iota of shame that we humans are fulfilling the Genesis 1:28 charge where our original dominion purpose has been revealed.

The Bible Is a Retrogressive Book More Than a Progressive Book

Generally speaking, through the eyes and spectacles of religion, the Bible is considered as the Word of God, which stipulates the laws and instructions that govern humanity and creation. And through this very Bible, creation develops and progresses effectively on earth. However, research and studies have shown me that the Bible is a retrogressive book before it can be progressive.

Once we assume dominion, we are introduced to our invisible divine source. So, one can easily say that the Bible is a book that sends us backward rather than forward. It's a retrogressive book that repositions humans to their original work assignment of dressing and keeping the earth as in Genesis chapter two.

When we fulfill our work assignment, then we have equally fulfilled our purpose assignment, that is, to take dominion over creation. The responsibility of dominion also means that we have tapped into our right source, which is God. So the Bible goes back more than it goes forward.

After all, the rest of the scriptural verses are restorative Scriptures and the prefix "re" means to be done again or repeated one more time. Anything that has the power to restore sends us back to the position of origination. Therefore, this proves that the Bible is a retrogressive book for our purpose dominion and not a progressive one unto religious rituals.

Our Ambassadorial Mandate Instructs Us to Reconcile and Reconnect People Back to God and Not Forward into Religions

So, when we have saved people from their disobedience, we must be able to direct them back to the original purpose of dominion where they are considered as rulers, controllers, teachers, masters, directors, and authoritative kings of the earth. If we don't, then the vision of God for the earth is not complete. We should not produce religious derelicts. Instead, we should help produce kingdom citizens who have the spirit of positive visions.

The Church Manifests God's Intentions, Will, and Purpose on Earth

God has outsourced His vision through us in order for us to become controllers of the earth realm. He has done this through the church. And as the church or the "called out ones," we are the spectacles and the office of God on earth. Nothing can be done on earth unless it is through the church. From Genesis to Revelation it's made vivid that Heaven never invades the earth realm unless it is through the church.

The word church in this context and discussion can be projected to be a typological reference to an individual or a point that is consecrated to God's holy use. The church is the individual in your vicinity who the Lord has consecrated and set apart for Himself and the medium through which God's intent and purpose get manifested. It is known that the church means a place or any point set aside for God to manifest His will, intent, and purpose on earth. Amos 3:7 (KJV) declares, "Surely the Lord GOD will do nothing, but he revealeth his secret unto his servants the prophets."

The Church Is the Light of the World

The church is always the light of the world. It's that lamp on a table or on a mountain that has given light to the darkness in the world. Who can imagine the world today without the church of God? It will be like a jungle where the law is eat or be eaten: "the survival of the fittest." "Do you not know that your body is the temple of the Holy Spirit…?" Paul exclaimed! (1 Corinthians 6:19). So, in the mind of God, He saves and encourages us to see ourselves as the mobile dominion agents. We don't go to church per se; rather, the church is in us and we walk into any established point to fellowship.

The Church Preaches the Message of the Kingdom

Jesus was the first perfect temple that walked on earth to share His visions and dreams of the sovereign kingdom. God has given every believer the vision of spreading this good news to the world too. That is one single reason why God established the church on earth. Every Christ-centered church must preach the message of the Kingdom of Heaven and the Kingdom of God (see Matthew 24:14). These two forces constitute the message of the Kingdom of God—His person and His destination.

This is the gospel we call good news. They are two separate things yet interrelated. The Kingdom of God is the person of a sovereign being and the Kingdom of Heaven is the destination and place of dwelling of a sovereign being. As the church on earth, we must preach both the Kingdom of God and the Kingdom of Heaven.

Most often in Jesus's messages, He preached one and the other depending on what He touched on at a time. It is the will of God for mankind to be saved and come to the knowledge of the truth, which is salvation through Jesus (see 1 Timothy 2:3-4). And we have instant salvation for the washing of all our acts of disobedience in our refusal of Jesus Christ, as the only means to dominion restoration. It's after the instant salvation experiences that we can then confess our acts of sin, which are revealed in our daily actions.

Salvation Does Not Come through the Confession of Sinful Acts

I must say that there is no salvation for any person in the world who confesses his sinful acts without first dealing with the roots of sin. The root of our sin is now the sin of refusing Christ as one's Lord and Savior. And the only person qualified to confess sinful acts is the person who has accepted Christ as Lord and Savior, and the rudiments of a cruel world entrap him into sin again.

Until the believer (the church) carries this responsibility, the religious movements will take over and prepare humans to Hell instead of Heaven. Every believer must uphold this vision and key of the Kingdom and open the floodgates of mercy for the world God so loved. We cannot afford to fail! We are His vision and the vision is to spread the Word.

My Personal Definitions of the Church

The church refers to a selected or elected body of persons who have been conditioned with an ambassadorial mind-set and kingdom concept; and they are assigned to influence the earth realm with these philosophies so that the entire earth region and its population will think and behave like the beings in Heaven where these concepts and ideas come from.

The church is Christ and Christ is the church. He's the Head and we are the body and together the picture of the total body is seen. Hence, the believer, who is part of the body, is interwoven and knitted together as one and cannot separate from Christ and vice versa. In this case, nobody can enter Heaven without the church. Never separate Christ from the church because they are inseparable.

The Specific Vision Assignments of Biblical Heroes

It is interesting to mention that the Bible offers us the opportunity to know that there were great heroes in history. We must never forget that every individual has a specific vision and purpose, so will be the way he or she functions.

For example, Moses was called to deliver the Israelites from the hand of the tyrant leader (pharaoh) of Egypt. Joseph being sold into slavery by his brothers was designed to save his family during the seven years of famine in Egypt, which also affected Canaan where Jacob, his father, was. Nehemiah was called for the repairs of the broken walls of Jerusalem. Paul was called to preach to the Gentiles, while Peter was sent to preach the good news to the Jews.

The list of great men and women of God who performed specific functions for God cannot be exhausted. Solomon was called for the building of the temple of God. David, his father, was called to deliver the Israelites from the hand of the Philistines and he was also a great musician as well as a dancer. Every child of God is called for one thing or the other and that particular thing becomes your vision. You must not fail to use your talent, which is the key to release and realize your vision for the glory of God.

Every leader you admire and respect today must have followed his vision and gifts consistently before becoming what he or she is presently. I pray that you discover your vision and gifts and use them to the glory of our God Almighty. Amen.

VISION POINTS

1. Each local church must have a specific vision apart from the general vision of the universal church.

2. Every Christ-centered church must preach Christ and His crucifixion.

3. The church is the vision of God for the world, an agency by which the world will be reconciled back to God.

4. Every single soul in the church fits in with a specific and definite purpose through their developed vision.

5. Discover your vision in your church.

6. Leadership comes about as a result of the power of vision in some men and its fulfillments.

7. Any leader or person you admired is an achiever and a success because of the pursuit of a vision.

WISDOM WORD

"Vision is the world's most desperate need. There are no hopeless situations, only people who think hopelessly."

—Winfred Newman

Chapter 9

DON'T BE DISOBEDIENT TO HEAVENLY VISIONS

And Samuel said, Hath the LORD as great delight in burnt offerings and sacrifices, as in obeying the voice of the LORD? Behold, to obey is better than sacrifice, and to hearken than the fat of rams. For rebellion is as the sin of witchcraft, and stubbornness is as iniquity and idolatry. Because thou hast rejected the word of the LORD, he hath also rejected thee from being king.
—1 Samuel 15:22-23 KJV

In Acts 26:19 (KJV), Apostle Paul said something that stresses the importance of obedience, particularly divine instruction: "Whereupon, O king Agrippa, I was not disobedient unto the heavenly vision." Here Paul confirms that there is a heavenly vision other than a personal vision and most people can be disobedient to it.

The proof of one's obedience is the positive and authentic decision one takes toward any important God-directed instruction. And the proof of disobedience is the negative decision one takes toward a God-given instruction. One can be obedient or disobedient to every heavenly vision based on one's decisions. Nothing precedes decision but one's own attitudes. Decision is the key to obedience and disobedience in life.

A right decision taken toward any heavenly vision then becomes our assignment mandates on earth. So you may ask, Pastor Oppong Amoabeng, what is my assignment? Your assignment in life is considered as your ability to make effective decisions to any God-given vision and purpose.

Samuel said to Saul that it is better to obey than to sacrifice because disobedience to heavenly visions is tantamount to rebellion and stubbornness is equal to witchcraft and idolatry. God wants His people to eat of the best of the lands in which they dwell, so He has instructed us by the words of prophet Isaiah, "If ye be willing and obedient, ye shall eat the good of the land: But if ye refuse and rebel, ye shall be devoured" (Isaiah 1:19-20a KJV).

What one sees and the decision one makes can help release a great measure of passion and enthusiasm for its achievement, and it matters little on one's former state of life. No success-oriented visionary ever gets limited and bound as a result of his past experience, self-inadequacies, and fear for the future. Paul, known as Saul, was a persecutor of the early Christians. Before his conversion, he was operating on his own vision of eradicating all Christians. This was not, however, God's vision for him. He had a wrong or satanic vision, which if not for the grace of Jesus he would have died a sinner. And if he had lived in this generation, he would have been labeled as a terrorist. Paul, we know today in biblical history, was one of the greatest Apostles of Jesus Christ after all that mess. He was learned and had all the energy and zeal to execute his satanic vision of persecuting Christians, but when he had the encounter with Jesus on his way to Damascus, he submitted himself to the heavenly vision.

The key to victory in life is a person's ability to submit in all meekness to the instructions God shows him or her and nothing whatsoever can impede the progress of this individual other than his own internal struggles. Vision gives assignments to men who can submit to God's will and equally take reasonable decisions to follow God, no matter the circumstances.

Don't be disobedient to the vision of God for you because the result is always disastrous. Take for example the disobedience of our first parents—Adam and Eve. By transgressing, they lost the Garden of Eden that God specially made for their enjoyment. It did not end there. It also brought death and all kinds of sufferings, which we are passing through to date as their descendants.

It is clear that where one stands in the divide of spiritual life and divinity suggests who he is and where he will be on any assignment, whether for the devil or for God. Relating this issue of obedience and disobedience, we can consider King Saul and Saul of Tarsus of the Old and New Testaments, respectively. The first king of Israel was Saul, just as the persecutor of the early church was Saul.

Both men were given specific visions or assignments to carry out by God in their respective generations. But King Saul out of arrogance and greed took a decision to disobey God, while Saul of Tarsus, on the other hand, took a decision not to be disobedient. So, after his conversion on the way to Damascus, Saul of Tarsus, who was also known as Paul (see Acts 13:9), decided to abandon his evil ways and embrace a heavenly vision that transformed him into becoming an Apostle of Christ. No wonder we have the common adage today saying that "Paul, who arrived late, has become greater than those he came to meet."

> *Saul, Saul, why persecutest thou me? it is hard for thee to kick against the pricks…I am Jesus whom thou persecutest. But rise, and stand upon thy feet: for I have appeared unto thee for this purpose, to make thee a minister and a witness both of these things which thou hast seen, and of those things in the which I will appear unto thee; Delivering thee from the people, and from the Gentiles, unto whom now I send thee, To open their eyes, and to turn them from darkness to light, and from the power of Satan unto God, that they may receive forgiveness of sins, and inheritance among them which are sanctified by faith that is in me.* (Acts 26:14c-18 KJV)

We should remember that both passive and active forms of disobedience are considered as total disobedience. And any time you disobey God you permit the devil to take advantage and mock God for His failure in your circumstance. We should know that the greatest pleasure and joy of God is to see His children in absolute and resolute obedience to His laws and visions. The best way to shame the devil is to render total obedience to the Word of God. Visionaries who succeed in their visions are said to be obedient people. It's believed that they trust God and lean on Him more than on anything else in their lives.

What about you? Will you be like King Saul or be like the Apostle? Why not emulate Apostle Paul? You must be a follower of Paul to win in your vision endeavors. You can emulate him and achieve positive results. It doesn't matter what your past experiences are. We know it is difficult both to forget and to change them. But one can ignore and control their negative influences and strive to win the present and the future.

These past experiences, both the good and the bad ones, can help us understand our immediate or future efforts, which enable us to make positive realizations. You see, everyone has his past experiential records, something that is not limited in any way to one person alone. The wisest thing to do is to ignore and never discuss what you wish others would forget about your past. So feel free and stand for the Lord; God is interested and ready to help you if only you are willing to obey and do His will.

Can you forget about your past now and surrender yourself to God just like Apostle Paul did? Make yourself available to God and He will use you to His glory. George Müller, the great life changer, had serious past issues but he turned around and changed his world through his God-given vision. Forget about what people will say and do not allow pride to ruin your life. Forget about what you have gone through in this life. Your true value is not discovered in what you have gone through, rather in what you are made for.

Abraham Received God's Blessing Because He Obeyed the Vision

Abraham worked with the vision that God showed him according to Genesis 12:1-3 (KJV):

Now the LORD had said unto Abram, Get thee out of thy country, and from thy kindred, and from thy father's house, unto a land that I will shew thee: And I will make of thee a great nation, and I will bless thee, and make thy name great; and thou shalt be a blessing: And I will bless them that bless thee, and curse him that curseth thee: and in thee shall all families of the earth be blessed.

How many of us today could have sacrificed all the wealth in Abraham's father's house just to pursue the vision of God? We must understand that when we disobey God's vision and pursue our own vision or those of Satan or men, the consequences are more likely to be imagined than described.

The devil's vision for mankind led to the fall of Adam and Eve in the Garden of Eden (see Genesis 3:6). Worldly visions of men have brought untold hardships to many people today. Worldly visions are mere expectations that can be from parents, age-group associates, or even your own opinions. Be careful not to become a victim!

The Bible says that "many are the plans in a person's heart, but it is the LORD'S purpose that prevails" (Proverbs 19:21 NIV). It is the counsel of the Lord that will stand in every vision of your heart. It is a fruitless effort to embark on a satanic, worldly, or personal vision other than that of God. We can get a clear example from the story of Babel, which we have discussed in the previous chapters.

Nimrod's Babel was self-centered and that led to his self-worship, self-orders toward human idolatry, and fatal failure. There's a lesson to be learned here—people can have plans and visions, but it's always the counsel of the Lord that will stand. When one develops any pursuit and effort without God, it can backfire because it was not God's vision for him. One must seek and pursue God's vision, for that is the only way to succeed and come to ultimate happiness.

VISION POINTS

1. You operate in a wrong vision when you go outside the will of God.

2. You can be disobedient to heavenly visions.

3. Blessings come one's way when he or she obeys God's vision.

4. Pursue God's vision for your life.

5. In life, it is always the vision of the Lord that will stand.

6. Your true value is not what you have gone through but what you are made for.

7. Obedience or disobedience is founded on an individual's personal decision making.

WISDOM WORD

"You were not meant for a mundane and mediocre lifestyle on earth. You must learn passionately to revive your passion for living on the earth. Be convinced to pursue your God-given dream, discover your purpose through your vision, and find your true life to your designed destination."
—A.O. Amoabeng

Chapter 10

EVERY MAN CAN OPERATE HIS GOD-GIVEN VISION

For God speaketh once, yea twice, yet man perceiveth it not. In a dream, in a vision of the night, when deep sleep falleth upon men, in slumberings upon the bed; Then he openeth the ears of men, and sealeth their instruction, That he may withdraw man from his purpose, and hide pride from man.

—Job 33:14-17 KJV

Do you know that you can discover, establish, celebrate, and succeed in your own God-designed and assigned vision? It is possible! It is true! You can establish every vision in your heart, no matter what the circumstances are. And when a person cultivates a fervent sensational burden that might probably be the vision God has instructed him or her with, when a person desires strongly to act on an idea, it may also be one of the ways one can realize his vision.

Persuasion is also another effective manner through which one can realize his or her vision. The ability to gather adequate knowledge on a particular subject matter or discipline can be a source of vision. The Bible says that "it is God who works in you both to will and to do for His good pleasure" (Philippians 2:13). Our visions are the pleasures of God through us.

One may also discover that sometimes people give up too early on an idea. They throw in the towel and give up. They will even discourage almost everybody concerning any ideas or projects. But you will still see a strong need to pursue such idea persuasively.

There are other culminating factors that help in realizing one's vision and we must put all in place and stick to the vision when it's noticed. Persistence, consistence, constancy, resistance, love and passion, strong desire for something, learning all about something, and habitual or routine interest in something, no matter the prevailing conditions, are some of the signs paramount to one's vision.

When one embarks on an idea with fervent joy and pleasure, we can also say that he has discovered his God-given vision. God has created each person for a purpose and that purpose is revealed through the vision that the individual perceives in his heart. A person's purpose is sealed with his vision and he must not allow what prevails around him to determine his fate. Anyone who wants to operate his vision should depend on his purpose and assignment through his individual gift, talent, and potential.

According to the Scriptures quoted above, God communicates visions and dreams to us in many ways: through revelations, reading and listening of the Word of God, association with people who can interpret our visions and dreams, prayers, sacrifices, among others. Oftentimes, when we sleep God sends instructions via our spirit in the form of dreams and visions. People who take their dreams very seriously can become high volume dreamers and those who give less consideration may end up as low volume or non-dreamers and automatically determine their vision. Consider Job 4:12-13 (KJV): "Now a thing was secretly brought to me, and mine ear received a little thereof. In thoughts from the visions of the night, when deep sleep falleth on men."

God Reveals Man's Purpose through Dreams and Visions

I personally got to know I was called for the work of the ministry through many other ways and timely through a major dream. It also brought deliverance and spiritual impartation to me as well. And God has on several occasions instructed and directed me in dreams and visions of the night.

As a visionary, I have learned how to respect the dreams I get and seek understanding from them because the interpretation of any dream is with the Lord and the confirmation of a dream is with the dreamer.

According to the Bible, the Holy Ghost is the last day ministerial dispensation in the calendar of Heaven, through which we will live lives of visions and dreams toward our purposes. The Bible can be divided into three major dispensations: Genesis to Prophet Malachi can be termed as the dispensation of the Father, Matthew to Acts 1 can be termed as the dispensation of Christ Jesus, and from Acts 2 to Revelation can be termed as the dispensation of the Holy Ghost. We are in the dispensation of the Holy Ghost and a vibrant believer cannot go without dreams and visions. The presence of the Holy Ghost is the era and proof of high-volume dreams and visions. And we can gain fervent insights and effective lifestyles through His impartation and blessing.

One major occurrence now is the super flow and abundance of dreams and visions to all flesh, both young and old, men and women and the entire human race (see Joel 2:28-29). The purpose of these dreams and visions thus facilitates the fulfillment of the purposes and assignments of our lives easier and faster than previous dispensations. And this means that you can fulfill any dream and vision inside you, no matter how big and great it appears.

Of course, God will always give you a dream and vision bigger and greater than yourself. Every dream and vision of God is bigger and greater than the people He calls on assignment. So if one is waiting for a smaller dream and vision, one must count himself out of the race of visions and purposes.

Satan Has a Vision for You, so Be Careful!

Satan also gives men vision, but his vision is contrary to God's will and His Word. Satan's vision is destructive and cruel and no man should endeavor to get it established. The most confusing element of all is that Satan uses the Word of God to perpetrate his desires and it's seen in his ability to quote, "it is written," and twist Scriptures to suit his schemes and deceits (see Matthew 4:5-6).

Satanic visions are negative and destructive. Second Timothy 3:1-10 reveal the results of satanic visions in the lives of men in the last days in which we are now. Of such examples we all know of, is the terrorist attack of the twin towers in New York (9/11) and the culminated numerous attacks in various parts of the world. It is Satan's vision to kill and destroy innocent people through ignorant people.

Humanity fights and destroys humanity when Satan takes charge of some human hearts and minds. There are certain human acts that create tension and problems in the world due to satanic invasions of human hearts; examples of which are the acts of terrorism that create divisions and polarizations among once united people.

Notwithstanding these, there are other minor evils we involve ourselves in for which Satan takes the pleasure for their establishment. The pleasure of Satan is the pain of God and the pleasure of God is the pain of Satan. God takes pleasure in our obedience and His greatest pain is when we disobey Him. We should be strong and vigilant as believers to see to it that we obey God at all times.

Life Without God's Vision Is Worthless and Meaningless

A man without the active presence of God's established vision is worthless like a lion among the company of sheep. A story is told of a baby lion captured by a shepherd. He tamed the lion in the pen of sheep until it began to behave like one. One day, from the nearby forest emerged a lion. The lion roared and the tamed "sheep-lion" fled for shelter.

It fled because it had no self-realization and discovery because for him, he was still more of a sheep than a lion. In real life, we are not what our frame/body portrays more than what our hearts portray.

The "sheep-lion" had not discovered its true self and make-up, that's why it feared though it had discovered the right association needed.

Finally, it decided to learn from that animal similar to it, only to discover for itself that all the while it was living below its true capacity and expectation. It needs a higher requirement in life to be the king of the forest. This story conveys a message of hope that we must rise to be what we are made to be and not conform to what we have been made to believe as a result of any condition. A person without a vision is like this "sheep-lion" who had a worthless and meaningless view for its life vision and purpose because it had not discovered what it really was.

You must capture the vision required of you, not expectations from circumstantial issues or public opinion. Nothing should condition and make you to compromise. God is good when your vision is God-given. He will supply resources to see to the actualization of your vision. God's vision always builds and restores lives and this is why we should all discover our true self and establish the dreams and visions of our lives toward our ordained purposes and assignments.

Vision Creates Order

Orderliness is proof of decorum, good orientation, and excellence. The proof of orderliness is the right act in a person's life. The absence of orderliness creates disorder. Disorder is a proof of lack of vision and where there is no vision, there is division. In the absence of vision and unity, there is division, confusion, conflicts, and quarrels. God gives vision to all who fear Him to terminate divisions. But the devil gives confusion to those he is able to deceive and breaks the cord of a visionary's vision. The confusion we see everywhere today even in the church is as a result of satanic visions, which bring kingdom divisions.

Visionaries Can Differentiate Vision Paradigms

Visionaries can differentiate vision paradigms. The great danger is when carnal men are unable to differentiate between God's vision and those of Satan because Satan has so transformed into an angel of light (see 2 Corinthians 11:14). Men of little faith can fall victims to his schemes. Spirit-led Christians can equally discern the presence of Satan and his active sense in any issue of life.

God is aware of Satan's activities everywhere and for that matter, He alerts His faithful servants to be ready to resist him as they submit to God. This ensures the flight of Satan as he flees from us and we can then establish our kingdom vision. In Job 1:6-7, it is written that Satan entered into the presence of God together with other angels who were unaware of his visit until God spotted him.

Verse 7 says, "And the LORD said to Satan, 'From where do you come?' So Satan answered the LORD and said, 'From going to and fro on the earth, and from walking back and forth on it.'"

In the same manner that Satan pretends to be an angel of light in the presence of God, he comes into the church to deceive God's children with the intention to steal, kill, and destroy (see John 10:10a). How does he steal, kill, and destroy? He does it through many ways, including divisions, backbiting, hatred, quarrels, arguments, and many more; you name it. The church is not spared from the devil's schemes and devices, so we must be vigilant! We must all heed to the advice of Paul in 1 Corinthians 10:12 (KJV) when he said, "Wherefore let him that thinketh he standeth take heed lest he fall."

Where There Is No Vision People Fight, Backbite, and Cause All Forms of Confusions

Because the devil is in charge of the things happening within and around, you can tell the kind of vision you are involved in. No wonder the Bible said, "You will know them by their fruits" (Matthew 7:16a). Apostle Paul goes ahead to list these fruits of the devil and those of the Holy Spirit of the living God in Galatians 5:19-23 (NIV):

The acts of the flesh [those of sinful nature] *are obvious: sexual immorality, impurity, and debauchery; idolatry and witchcraft; hatred, discord, jealousy, fits of rage, selfish ambition, dissensions, factions and envy; drunkenness, orgies, and the like. I warn you, as I did before, that those who live like this will not inherit the kingdom of God.* [These are devilish visions for humans.] *But the fruit of the Spirit* [which is the vision of God for His children] *is love, joy, peace, forbearance, kindness, goodness, faithfulness, gentleness and self-control. Against such things there is no law.*

This simply means that if you neglect to operate on these visions of God, you are on your own and you cannot blame God for anything that happens. We must continually watch and pray in order not to allow Satan to have access to the church to cause divisions and other forms of confusions. When you are steadfast to God's vision for your life, Satan has no other choice than to leave you to do the work of your God who has called you. I am a living example of this testimony.

When the Lord called me for ministerial assignment, there were pressures from different quarters. But I thank God that I did not fall prey to any. I started to gather people until I was planted with my family. When I took that great step of faith most people left, leaving behind my wife, my daughter, and my mother-in-law. I have never completely understood what led to that circumstance, but there is one major thing I know—never to give up on my vision and dream.

I refused to give up because I believed the Lord who spoke to me was faithful to recreate my old world into a new world. I know that whoever God calls He equips for a specific work for specific and definite people and today, the testimony has come to limelight. Thank God for His grace and love! Great folks of noble minds are gathered around this vision and we are running it successfully.

For you to accomplish your God-given vision, you must heed God's voice rather than any other voice. Saul listened to the voice of men and that brought his fall as the first king of Israel. Aaron also did the same thing and he led the great nation of Israel astray into idol worship, idol creation, and idol fellowshipping. You must be careful as you operate on your vision and dream.

If you are operating on God's vision, you must be ready to obey the voice of God since He holds the keys and principles that effectively help to establish a dream. One must follow any direction He takes because He knows where He is taking you. No wonder the Bible says God orders the steps of the righteous man (see Psalms 37:23). He can never mislead you, because your success is His joy and you cannot afford to disappoint Him.

When God has made His vision clear to you, all you need is to begin to operate it because you know where you are going, what you're supposed to do, when to do it, how to do it, why you must do it, and what it must result in. God makes all these clear to you and it is discovered before you embark in the journey of pursuing the positive power of vision.

VISION POINTS

1. Satan can have access to your God-given vision when you become carnal-minded.

2. The devil's vision is to steal, kill, and destroy the purposes of God in your life.

3. As you walk in the Spirit and exhibit the fruits of the Spirit, your vision will live with you and not leave you.

4. When you are steadfast and strong, Satan has no other choice than to leave you to do the work of your God.

5. The ability to stand in the wake of attacks on your vision gives credence to the fact that you are tough and moving ahead with your vision.

6. Things happening within you and around can tell the kind of vision you are operating on.

7. Currently, there is a superabundance of dreams and visions because of the dispensation of the Holy Ghost.

8. Spirit-led visionaries can always differentiate vision paradigms and discern satanic vision from kingdom vision.

9. God reveals our purpose through dreams and visions on our night beds.

10. Life without God's vision and purpose is worthless and meaningless.

WISDOM WORD

"A visionary must live and die for something. Things you live for die for you, and things you die for live for you."

—A. O. Amoabeng

Chapter 11

TIPS FOR A SUCCESSFUL VISION

There is no fast track to success. Success is a process that is progressive and it takes clear vision to realize each step of this process; it also takes the same vision; kindled by prayer, passion, possibility attitude, patience, and persistence to achieve good success in life.

—Claude Mann

In the previous chapters, we noticed these unveiling prerequisites: whenever God reveals His vision, He equally releases a gift, an idea, and a principle to the recipients, which ensures accomplishment of purposes. He also makes everything clear to us and gives us room to ask questions regarding that vision.

Humanly speaking, we may be feeble, but we should be able to initiate action-steps toward any divine assignment boldly without relenting whatsoever. As it is revealed in the passages of the Bible, Moses for example, asked God questions that equally revealed his humanity. Any person who knows God also realizes his or her human weakness and cries out for His divine abilities. Moses asked God about his inadequacies and inabilities and cried out for divine support.

Joshua was instructed to be bold and courageous, meaning that he was afraid to assume the mantle of leadership after the death of Moses. Jeremiah resorted to the fear of childhood delinquencies. Gideon had no faith in his personality. So it is normal to me when one becomes afraid to produce the action-steps God has mandated the individual to fulfill.

Our lives' visions and purposes are far bigger, and they outweigh our personal ambitions, our self-cultivated initiatives, and our strong desires. Therefore, anytime God reveals His heart's plan for a person, it's likely that the individual will exclaim, "Oh Lord, I am weak, small, or unable to do it." God's purpose is far greater than our wildest dream, personal connections, education, and possession.

His purpose is that the inner equipment of the human comes out of him through the power of vision. Everyone is absolutely equipped and empowered with all that it takes to make any dream achievable without the support of any external factor. Rather, our potential attracts external things toward us for our personal advantage and advancement.

God does not want you to be found wanting in any way as a visionary. That is why He has deposited potentials, talents, and gifts in you. Your gift will make you great and bring you before great people. Where you lack the knowledge of the way, your gift and talent will make a way for you. I was nobody until I discovered my gifts and talents. This has changed me dramatically into a more focused and morally balanced individual.

We search within ourselves to be whatever God has ordained us to be and not vice versa. Proverbs 18:16 (KJV) declares, "A man's gift maketh room for him, and bringeth him before great men." This is because "a gift is as a precious stone in the eyes of him that hath it: whithersoever it turneth, it prospereth" (Proverbs 17:8 KJV). Hence, one's ability to recognize, appreciate, and celebrate his own gifts, talents, and potentials, turns him to be a prosperous person no matter what kind of external factor may becloud him. When we execute our vision effectively, it produces seven dimensions of prosperity.

A) Physical (see 3 John 1:2)

B) Occupational (see Psalms 107:37-38)

C) Marital (see Hebrews 13:4; Proverbs 18:22)

D) Spiritual (see Ezekiel 36:26)

E) Financial (see Proverbs 10:22)

F) Mental (see Isaiah 26:3)

G) Social (see Luke 1:40-52)

When we are blessed with prosperity, we also move to the highest dimension of seven potent elevations in Christ Jesus (see Revelation 5:12). They are:

1. Power

2. Riches

3. Wisdom

4. Strength

5. Honor

6. Glory

7. Blessing

The aforementioned, help every individual on earth to become successful and rise to the height of glory and comfort. They help us to fulfill our lives' dreams and purposes. It's imperative to understand this secret—God doesn't always need our school certificates to release our potential, talent, or gift. But He needs the awareness of our inherent abilities to advance us. As visionaries, there are basic subjective questions we often ask ourselves of which God provides answers before we recognize and celebrate our vision orientations. The following are questions that are common to us.

What Am I Supposed to Do?

THE vision is of God, and therefore you must remember what God asked you to do. And what He showed you to do was given in invisible and indelible language form and your obedience in developing a written form guides your vision action. The Holy Spirit enables vision-aries to remember all a visionary has been taught or instructed to do. He gives His Word and tells us what to do with the Word. We work with the God of the Word in our vision career and not just working the Word to work for us. This is because when one learns how to walk with God and apply His Word, manifestation becomes an inevitable reality and God takes the glory.

The purpose of every God-given vision is meant to transform the mind from a negative doubtful thinking-manner to a positive faith-thinking one. It's never enough to have all kinds of ideas in the mind and rarely put them in practice. How serious we become in our designated purposes and visions determines how we will see ourselves.

Visionaries identify their assignment as their identity. Oftentimes, when I read I wonder why some characters like John the Baptist never showcased his parental background but his purpose assignment when the Pharisees asked of it. John the Baptist only introduced himself by his purpose and not by his family creed. We can learn a very good and important lesson from this. From the principle or method of John, we must be able to tell people who we are in Christ Jesus more than any other identification.

He sought himself out from the Word of God. He introduced him-self as the one crying out in the wilderness who was preparing the way for the Lord (see John 1:22-23). Wow! The man didn't say, "I am the son of Zachariah, the priest, and Elizabeth, the pious woman." He was his purpose mandate and all other possible introductions came as second-ary issues. Visionaries speak their purpose assignment as their identity and not the other way. They speak the Word and work the Word for every situation that confronts them.

Who Will Help Me Carry out This Dream to Completion?

The vision is of God, and He has made every provision for it. As it was cited in the case of Zerubbabel, "The hands of Zerubbabel [h]ave laid the foundation of this temple; His hands shall also finish it" (Zechariah 4:9a-b). No matter the set odds and difficulties, you have been anointed to start and to complete the work in your hands.

Your dream is like a magnet that attracts the same kind of human elements to it. They will come from the four cardinals of the earth and give the needed support. As in the case of Moses, he had Aaron and Miriam; David had Jonathan; Jesus had twelve disciples; Elijah had Elisha; and Elisha had Gehazi; Abraham had Lot; and Noah had his three sons.

At the moment, I can be used as a case study because I have some great people around me who are helping me to achieve the vision. They are helping to accomplish God's endeavors and projects through which they equally get fulfilled. So you see, you too have somebody around you. Just learn how to recognize and share the fellowship of coordination or cooperation and your dream will be accomplished in due time.

How Will I Do It?

The vision is of God and it has been given with specific and definite instructions. These instructions must be respected and adhered to. And the visionary must be surrounded with positive thinkers, encouragers, sponsors, and people with expertise and skill needed to steer the vision to the desired end.

However, I must be strong on this, that visionaries must be ready to protect the language of the vision and they should allow the team players to use their respective and combined skills and definite knowledge to execute the plans of the vision. In 2 Chronicles 2:11b-14, the king of Tyre, Hiram, replied to King Solomon with these gracious words of encouragement and blessing,

> *Because the LORD loves His people, He has made you king over them…Blessed be the LORD God of Israel, who made heaven and earth, for He has given King David a wise son, endowed with prudence and understanding, who will build a temple for*

the LORD and a royal house for himself! And now I have sent a skillful man, endowed with understanding, Huram my master craftsman (the son of a woman of the daughters of Dan, and his father was a man of Tyre), skilled to work in gold and silver, bronze and iron, stone and wood, purple and blue, fine linen and crimson, and to make any engraving and to accomplish any plan which may be given to him, with your skillful men and with the skillful men of my lord David your father.

I believe that every visionary should adopt and learn these principles and methods of these great kings.

Why Should I Do It?

There is a purpose for every vision under the Heavens and that is the reason one must execute the vision with all the heart, mind, and soul. In the first place, the vision is of God and everything that is of God is good and perfect. Living without a dream or vision is dangerous and that is why God has given you a definite and unique vision. God has wired your life for this very reason and you can't do without it.

You know deep in the heart that you were born for this course. Every person must come to his purpose assignment in life to be successful; everybody must know why he exists. Every person is a failure without a discovery of personal purpose plan from God. And whoever God calls, He equips with purpose, vision, might, and power.

You will know that this vision is God's original intent for your life when it begins to burn, cause inner sensations, and push your passions and enthusiasms to their ultimate. Every fiber of your being will respond to the heavenly vision and you will be ready to give up everything just to pursue and to fulfill this vision. Peter left fishing in the oceans for fishers of men in the oceans of worldliness and sin. Matthew left tax collection. Paul left the advocacy business. Luke left the medical field.

When you identify your purpose, everything else is absolutely irrelevant and nonsense. Nothing will be able to restrain you and nothing will make you happy except for your purpose. You will move ahead with dogged faith until you have seen the vision birthed. You will know and be motivated by the fact that it is this vision that will create your success on earth and finally your happiness; you will give glory to your God who has given you the vision.

The following information can help us to successfully realize our God-given vision.

1. One must be born again.

Many have misconceptions and misunderstandings of this born-again phraseology. The misunderstanding emerges because of the fanciful endeavors of religion to impeach the kingdom government concepts of God. Born-again is not a religious terminology and he who looks at it from that point deviates drastically. Rather, it is a kingdom phraseology, which despises sin because God has already marginalized or negated its influence and potency over humanity.

We don't confess our sins and become saved. We call on the name of the Lord by confessing his Christhood and lordship over our lives in order to be saved. We confess Christ and we are saved. We don't confess sins as sinners and are saved. Sinners are disqualified from confessing their sins because they cannot be forgiven that way. A sinner confesses Christ Jesus for instant salvation. The only people qualified to confess their sins are believers. Unbelievers should not confess their sins because they are living in sin. They must rather confess Jesus Christ as the Lord and Savior before they can ever confess their private and personal sins.

We confess Christ Jesus for our instant salvation and we confess our sins for our progressive and ultimate salvation. As believers, we are saved instantly by our confession of Christ. We are in the process of being saved because every day we are working out our own salvation in fear and trembling as we discipline ourselves to lay apart filthiness and superfluity in naughtiness and receive with meekness the Word of God, which saves our souls (see Philippians 2:12; James 1:21).

The visionary must know that as believers we are saved, we are being saved, and we will be saved. The confession of sins has its place in our lives, but it can't be considered above the confession of Christ in relationship to our instant salvation. Sin has been dealt with before we sinned. But what must be dealt with in unbelievers now is their refusal and disobedience to accept Jesus Christ as the only way and truth into coming back to God.

The born-again phraseology simply means the repentance and ultimate acceptance and confession of the Lord Jesus Christ as one's Lord and personal Savior so that the person can be reinstated, reestablished, reintroduced, and returned to his source in God and to become the dominion agent once again on the earth.

So it is an advantage to be born-again and not a disadvantage. Having been born-again means you are now available for God's use to realize His purpose for creating you. God's purpose for creating man is to relate to us as we work out His work of dominion on the earth. Two main reasons unfold as purposes behind our creation. The first is for the purpose of fellowship and relationship between God and us. And the second is for the purpose of occupation. No doubt, we know that purpose is the center of living on earth. Moreover, God takes pleasure in His creation when we fulfill the reason for our living. Therefore, I can comfortably say that when God gives man vision, His purpose is that man will discover the purpose of his life through that given vision and improve upon life and progress.

2. One must know and discover his vision.

The first step into discovering your vision is the awareness that every single person on earth must walk in his or her God-given vision that leads to his God-given purpose. Vision is a vehicle that transports you to your purpose in life. You have your purpose already but you need to see into your vision for your purpose to get accomplished. You may ask, "How can I know my vision?" Simple, every human being has been gifted in one way or the other by God (see Ephesians 4:7-8), and it is your duty to find out what your unique gift is. How do I find out my gift? Pray and seek the face of God. We are empowered through the statement of Jesus Christ in Luke 11:9-10 (NIV): "Ask and it will be given to you; seek and you will find; knock and the door will be opened to you. For everyone who asks receives; the one who seeks finds; and to the one who knocks, the door will be opened."

This Scripture dispels the notion that God's children have no reason for not realizing their visions because our Creator is ready at any time to help us as Jesus has revealed to us. Everything God made is for a purpose, so discover your vision as you make your request known unto God. And the peace of God, which transcends all understanding, will guard your hearts and your minds in Christ Jesus (see Philippians 4:7).

3. One must guide against worldly influences on his vision.

The living Word of God in you must protect your vision. When the Word of God is in you, the "world" goes out of you and vice versa. There are no neutral grounds for the Word and the world. You definitely belong to one of them. Much as the Word can influence you and take the world out of you, the world can likewise do the same. Your position determines your allocation and disposition. Location has power to suggest your allocation.

As you harness your God-given vision, be careful of those you call "friends." Many will pretend to be real friends. Many people will pretend they are for you, but in a real sense, they may be your foes. A friend is supposed to be for you. Most so-called friends are dangerous pythons and adders. They bite in secret places and destroy your good reputation with evil flavors. They pretend they are for you but they are actually against you. The truth is, this is what vision does. Vision creates divisions, additions, subtractions, and multiplications. As you move on to implement your vision, do not be surprised of what you hear from men who are against your vision.

Choose your associates with prudence and with great discernment. Be steadfast in your prayers, so that the anointing on you will in turn break any weapon fashioned against you. I experienced this at the beginning of my ministry. Evil forces fought against the dream from different quarters, but they never succeeded. The devil will never leave you; he will repeatedly return to try to stop the move of God. However, be on guard and protect what God has given you. Especially if your vision is in the "teething stage," be careful whom you share it with. Speak less to men but speak all out to God and He will direct you on the right path. Today, I see that almost the entire vision God showed me to do is becoming a reality in my life. Every day a pile of glory is added, notwithstanding setbacks and difficulties. The dream is becoming a reality, and to Him be all the glory!

"Do not be deceived: 'Evil company corrupts good habits,'" says Apostle Paul (1 Corinthians 15:33). Always ask God to guide you to choose friends and associates in ministry or business. You need genuine friends who are friends in need and friends indeed. Crosscheck any advice from friends with God's Word before application because sometimes the devil can use them to shatter your plans. Let me take this opportunity and share one such dangerous advice that I received from a friend. Some time ago, in the initial church planting stages of Impact Temple, my family was going through some challenges, probably due to the poor view and understanding of the huge dynamics that go with vision versus small job incomes as a factory handed in a new tight system. Life was very difficult. I was paying for the church auditorium, paying for my house rent, utility bills, and many other responsibilities. My wife had also lost her job because she was nursing our daughter. A friend came to me and advised me to stop the building of the church and rather concentrate on my family's upkeep. She reasoned that I could always start again when things were okay and we had enough money. The advice seemed sincere, but as I reflected on it, I discovered that it was way out of God's will and was meant to sway me from my priority of putting God first. My vision was to build God's house first at all cost. We never get money to start a vision. But we can get money when we initiate a vision. Money comes for the vision through the vision declaration.

Look, in life what you put down as your priority is crucial for fulfilling your vision. If you want to succeed, develop the habit of making a priority list for everything you do and follow it. In your scale of preference, put God first and all things next. I did that. I went ahead to obey God by building His house, in spite of my difficulty and today He has blessed me for what I did. Value God's voice above all other voices in your life.

4. One must listen to God for direction.

Do not rely on your ability. Ability is sometimes deceptive. Sometimes you may think you have all it takes to have a successful vision, but without God all the efforts will come to naught. That is why in Proverbs 16:1-3, the Bible says we may make our plans, but God has the last word. You may think everything you do is right, but the Lord judges your motives. Ask the Lord to bless your plans, and you will be successful in carrying them out.

The King James Version renders it this way, "The preparations of the heart in man, and the answer of the tongue, is from the LORD. All the ways of a man are clean in his own eyes; but the LORD weigheth the spirits. Commit thy works unto the LORD, and thy thoughts shall be established." This is the advice Solomon has given to anyone who wants to succeed. Also, in Proverbs 3:5-6 (KJV) Solomon said, "Trust in the LORD with all thine heart; and lean not unto thine own understanding. In all thy ways acknowledge him, and he shall direct thy paths." Permit God to oversee your efforts and affairs. He knows the way and He will lead you to success.

5. One must not be in a hurry to realize his vision.

There is time for everything. The fulfillment of your vision depends on time and only God decides the time. Acts 1:7 (KJV) speaks to the fact that God controls our time and hence how your vision must get accomplished: "It is not for you to know the times or the seasons, which the Father hath put in his own power." Galatians 4:4a-b says, "But when the fullness of the time had come, God sent forth His Son." Your vision will be fulfilled and the purpose for existing will come to pass when God's timing is considered.

Do not compare your vision with another's. You may have what looks like a similar vision with another person, but the timing and methods of fulfillment may differ. Trust in God and wait. Don't rush your vision at all. For example, God called Moses to build a temple (the tabernacle) in the wilderness, but was it the same as the temple He asked Solomon to build? They were never the same. Again, the method by which Samson killed the lion wasn't the same as the method David used to kill them. Abraham went to Egypt when there was famine, but Isaac was asked to stay in the land of famine and sow his seed. Prophet Elijah raised the dead by lying prostrate over the body, while our Lord Jesus Christ raised the dead by simply commanding the dead to come forth. General Naaman was healed of leprosy by dipping himself seven times in the Jordan River, while Miriam was placed outside the camp to be healed. So who said methods and ways are the same? They are inexhaustible.

God has methods as well as timing for every vision given to His children. Never worry when your own is not yet fulfilled. It is not over until God says it is all over. Believe God, He will never disappoint you.

6. One must be humble.

Humility is the first law in Heaven. Proverbs 22:4 says that humility and the fear of the Lord bring wealth and honor in life. Great men and women of God we know in life today achieved those feats because they were and are considered as humble people. God opposes the proud. When you are proud, God has nothing to do with you. Apostle Paul advised us in Philippians 2:5-11 (NASB) to imitate our Lord Jesus Christ:

> *Have this attitude in yourselves which was also in Christ Jesus, who, although He existed in the form of God, did not regard equality with God a thing to be grasped, but emptied Himself, taking the form of a bond-servant, and being made in the likeness of men. Being found in appearance as a man, He humbled Himself by becoming obedient to the point of death, even death on a cross. For this reason also, God highly exalted Him, and bestowed on Him the name which is above every name, so that at the name of Jesus EVERY KNEE WILL BOW, of those who are in heaven and on earth and under the earth, and that every tongue will confess that Jesus Christ is Lord, to the glory of God the Father.*

Humble People Do Great Things

The key to elevation is humility and pride comes before destruction. Through humility, these people obeyed God's calling and achieved great things in their lives. For instance, God called Oral Roberts to build a university and he humbled himself and obeyed. God used him mightily to heal many bodies and minds and he is considered as a father of faith today.

So is evangelist Billy Graham. He was called to evangelize and win souls for God. Kenneth Copeland and Dr. Creflo Dollar lead the church to fight poverty by teaching kingdom principles for achieving prosperity. Myles Munroe taught leadership principles, purpose assignments among people in the developing nations, and transformed followers to become leaders. Mother Teresa is perhaps the greatest woman the world has provided humanity, counting on her outstanding gift and compassionate passion for the poor. Mahatma Gandhi led a peaceful demonstration and overthrew the colonial government that sat upon their necks in India. In Africa, we can talk about Nelson Mandela of South Africa, Kwame Nkrumah and Kofi Annan of Ghana, Nnamdi Azikiwe and Wole Soyinka of Nigeria, among others.

All these are humble people who have obeyed and pursued their God-given visions and have been rewarded by the Lord Jesus. Pride destroys. Do not imitate Satan who out of pride has been ruined forever.

VISION POINTS

1. You must be born-again to realize your God-given vision.

2. You must know and understand the purpose of your vision.

3. Guide against worldly influences on your vision.

4. Seek and listen to directions you must take when you have a vision from God.

5. Don't rush your vision because visions get fulfilled by the appointed times of the Lord.

6. Humility pays more than being bossy, for if you humble yourself, God will lift you up in due course.

7. It is not over until God says it is over.

WISDOM WORD

"There is a difference between a visionary and a manager. Visionaries lead the way but managers manage what is available on the way. You need the compliments of both to fulfill the course of your vision."

—Dr. Afua Asabea Amoabeng

CONCLUSION

My dear reader, we have come to the end of the lessons in terms of reading this book and we are now going to look at the practical aspects of what we have learned. The biggest challenge is really discovered in real life while confronting situations; and therefore, we must make a conscious effort to practice the keys suggested in this book. The wise man says that it is easier said than done. Or that the day of planning is always different from the day of battle.

Battles are won step by step. A journey of a thousand miles begins with the first step. And little drops of water make a mighty ocean. The saying goes—the ball is in one's court—thus, as an individual visionary it is important to use all the available keys postulated and propounded to cultivate every important habit and attitude that will enable a person to operate in the elevated sense on earth as a dominion person.

I believe I have fairly done my part of the contract between us humans and God by allowing my thoughts to be arranged and packaged profitably to you as a channel through which your own God-purposed assignment will be achieved. God has blessed us with such a powerful instruction, crucial for our elevation. This is the main reason for my motivation and inspiration. Let it enlighten and inspire you! So, child of God, arise, run with your vision, pursue purpose, and achieve your God-given vision with passion, prayer, and persistence.

It is now your turn to put what you have just read into action. I agree that you have a personal life, but you don't have a private life.

Don't misconceive this truth; your personal life cannot disengage your private life as a leader. God will order only the steps you take, so do not stand still any longer. Write that vision. Pray over that vision and seek divine direction. Plan with that vision and begin pursuing your purpose. Life is the threefold cord of prioritization, organization, and discipline. Do not allow that dream to become a nightmare or a byword. Spark that vision and move ahead in faith, knowing that God Himself is with you in its pursuit.

Everything you have read in this book is written through the inspiration of the Holy Spirit. I am just a vessel and God can use anyone who avails himself. Look at me and begin this vision journey because I am a man who is himself pursuing a vision, just like you. We must all look to Jesus Christ who is "the **author** and **perfecter** of our faith" (Hebrews 12:2a ASV). He alone has seen it all and has been through it all. His vision took Him to the cross and even into the womb of the earth, but He did not remain in the tomb. He rose again! He is the resurrection and the life.

If He is with you in this journey of vision pursuit, you are blessed, for you are with the One who knows and sees the ending from the beginning. He knows you can succeed and sees the destination you are traveling to. That is why you must follow Him, one-step at a time as He unfolds the vision to you one phase after another. With Christ, your vision cannot die. With Christ, you shall not cast-off restraint because He has given you vision.

May the Holy Spirit illuminate your path with His living light and show you the right way to the right place of destiny the Father has established for your fulfillment. You can do it! Dare to dream and when you dream, dream big. Dare to see beyond the limitations. Choose to pursue excellence. Choose to live above sin and mediocrity. Let this book be a compass and the Holy Spirit will direct you as you apply the principles herein to actualize your vision.

Finally, my beloved, I pray for you that you may come to the full knowledge of your definite purpose in life and may you experience a never ceasing outpouring of the inspiration of the Holy Spirit.

May your life reflect Heaven on earth and may you receive grace from the Father to jump each hurdle of life and move ahead to fulfill that vision God has given you. May your heart be refreshed daily with faith, faithfulness, forgiveness, joy, passion, love, compassion, and with "fresh wine" for the greater works ahead of you, in Jesus's name, I pray for you! Amen. Shalom!

THE PRAYER OF REPENTANCE

Finally, friend, you have to pray the prayer of repentance. Normally, the church calls it the sinner's prayer. In this prayer, you want to make a life commitment to God through Jesus Christ. You want to make Jesus Christ your personal Savior and LORD. As you invite Him into your life, transformation and permanent change will come into your life. I did it one day and you will have to do it today. Tomorrow, they say, may be too late.

SAY PRAYERFULLY

"Dear Lord Jesus Christ, I have heard Your Word, and how You came to the earth, died, and resurrected for my salvation. You took my place and stood in the gab for my sins; I acknowledge this truth and repent for my refusal to accepting that You are Lord and Savior. Come into me because I believe what You did. I confess with my own mouth that You are Lord. Come into me and stay in me the rest of my life. In Jesus's name, I pray. Amen."

RENOUNCE AND DENOUNCE SATAN BOLDLY

"Satan, you once deceived me.

And it is enough!

I know my rights in Christ Jesus.

I am a purchased son of God.

I am rightly paid for by the blood of God's precious Lamb: Christ Jesus.

I have just accepted His gift of life.

So, from now onwards get out of my life.

You are demoted to your bondage.

I renounce and denounce your influence over my vision and purpose.

I am the son of God with full control on earth.

I bind you from my vision and purpose, my personal life and properties.

In the name of Jesus Christ, I am free forever and ever. Amen!"

ABOUT THE AUTHOR

Reverend Oppong Amoabeng is an ordained minister of the gospel and a prolific writer. He functions in an elevated sense of motivation and inspiration. From a humble beginning, he has risen to become a voice that influences people with a practical, down-to-earth kingdom mind-set teaching and preaching. He is the Resident Pastor of ICGC-Copenhagen, Denmark, and the Area Supervising Minister for ICGC-Europe.

Reverend Oppong Amoabeng is a sought-after speaker who travels widely and shares his insights at conferences, seminars, and church pulpits. The uniqueness of his message reveals his gifts and his God-given ability to deliver the Word of God undiluted so powerfully that it makes a great impact on the listeners. He is married to Mrs. Comfort Asantewaah Amoabeng and they are blessed with two daughters and two sons.

**For any information on the book or the author,
please contact any of the addresses below:**

OFFICE: Rentermastervej 691, 2TV 2400 NV, Copenhagen Denmark

TEL: +4531320559

E-MAIL: oarkbooks@yahoo.com/revamoabeng@gmail.com

FACEBOOK: Oppong Amoabeng/ICGC-MESSIANIC TEMPLE

BOOKS BY THE AUTHOR

- *IN PURSUIT OF DIVINE PROSPERITY.* In this book, the author writes that prosperity is the fruit of productivity. The blessed character prospers. Satan can also prosper humans. Prosperity is the highest wish of God for man. And that the church has no message to preach but prosperity. How we preach the message determines how it will fulfill or abuse purpose.

- *UNDERSTANDING THE LAWS OF DIVINE HEALING.* Published and distributed worldwide by Evangelista Media. It is a 160-page book on 20 principles that facilitate divine healing and provide health. The highest wish of God is for your health and healing. The author writes that there are basic practical steps of faith we take, and God responds with a miracle of healing.

- *THE JOURNEY OF SUCCESS.* A.O. Amoabeng instructs that success is not a destination, but a progressive journey of life. And God has invested eight things as a universal gift for humanity, which ensures our success. The way to success is the ancient pathways we follow. You do yourself a disservice if you don't succeed on earth.

- *THE POSITIVE POWER OF VISION.* This may probably be the best book on vision you may have read this year. A.O. Amoabeng hits it directly on the nail. This book is the surest way to operate in the elevated sense as a vision-ary. And highlights are made in this powerful book on the positive power of seeing. Everything you are seeing today may have a second spiritual meaning and interpretation for your personal elevation.

- *HOW FAR CAN YOU SEE?* How far we see is not determined or influenced by where we come from. Our approach to life is because of how we see. Achievers see far and you can be one of them. The author has stated diamonds in words and you can fly through this effective mechanism and reach your ultimate destination in life.

- *ORDAINED TO BREAKTHROUGH OPPOSITION* is a six killer identification of opposition. Above all, it is a strategic invasion weapon over the power of obstacles and Hell. This is a powerful 56-page secret you should never let go unread. You'll learn how to overcome the oppositions in your life and use them as success ingredients to prepare a recipe.

Publishing Services by
EVANGELISTA MEDIA & CONSULTING

Via Maiella, 1
66020 San Giovanni Teatino (CH) – Italy

publisher@evangelistamedia.com

www.evangelistamedia.com

 /evangelistamediaconsulting

 evangelista_media_consulting

SCAN THE QRCODE BELOW TO CONTACT US: